Achilles Rose

Christian Greece and living Greek

Achilles Rose

Christian Greece and living Greek

ISBN/EAN: 9783337167035

Printed in Europe, USA, Canada, Australia, Japan

Cover: Foto ©ninafisch / pixelio.de

More available books at **www.hansebooks.com**

CHRISTIAN GREECE

AND

LIVING GREEK

BY

Dr. ACHILLES ROSE

"Αἰσχρόν ἐστι σιγᾶν Ἑλλάδος πάσης ἀδικουμένης."

NEW YORK
PERI HELLADOS PUBLICATION OFFICE
126 East Twenty-ninth Street
1898

To

Mr. BERNARD G. AMEND

MY HIGHLY ESTEEMED FRIEND

THIS BOOK IS RESPECTFULLY DEDICATED

CONTENTS.

CHAPTER I.
An Historical Sketch of Greek, . . . 1

CHAPTER II.
The Proper Pronunciation of Greek, . . 40

CHAPTER III.
The Byzantines, ... 77

CHAPTER IV.
The Greeks Under Turkish Bondage, . . 131

CHAPTER V.
The Greek War of Independence and the European Powers, ... 168

CHAPTER VI.
The Kingdom of Greece Before the War of 1897, ... 195

CHAPTER VII.
Greek as the International Language of Physicians and Scholars in General, . 226

Epilogue, ... 269

A POLITICAL RETROSPECT ON GREECE.

THOSE who are now blaming defeated Greece for having gone to war against Turkey unprepared and without allies, "with surprising blindness and thoughtlessness" as the prime minister of one of the great powers put it, ought to take into consideration the peculiar and exceptional circumstances under which the present Greek kingdom has been laboring since its very creation in 1830. In the revolution of 1821, or rather the war of independence as the Greeks call it, not only Greece proper, but most of the islands of the Ægean Sea, Crete included, took up arms against Turkey. The revolution lasted nearly seven years, and ended with the Battle of Navarino in October, 1827, when thirty men-of-war of England, France, and Russia destroyed the Turkish and Egyptian fleets, composed of one hundred and twenty vessels, at that port. This great act, which sealed the independence of

Greece, and yet was called "an untoward event" by the Duke of Wellington, then Prime Minister of England, was due to the enthusiasm roused throughout the civilized world by the heroism of the Greeks, when the names of Marco Bozzaris, Canaris, Miaulis, Ypsilanti, Karaïskakis, Colocotronis, and others, were in everybody's mouth. But when the fixing of the frontiers of the new kingdom was being discussed, the jealousy of the great powers, with the exception of France, asserted itself as usual, and through the hostility of Prince Metternich, then Prime Minister of Austria, and the selfish policy of England under the Wellington ministry, Crete and most of the islands were ceded back to Turkey, and the new kingdom, scarcely containing eight hundred thousand souls, was made so small that Prince Leopold of Saxe-Coburg, afterwards king of the Belgians, refused the Greek throne which was offered to him by the powers.

Greece thus began her political existence with a restricted territory, devastated by the long war, and with very scant resources. But gradually the country commenced to thrive, notwithstanding so many disadvantages, most of which were an inheritance from its late masters; agriculture made great strides, a pretty large commerce was established with foreign countries, and a commercial marine, comprising over four thousand vessels (in 1850), almost monopolized the carrying trade of the Mediterranean, of the Black Sea, of the Sea of Azoff, and of the lower Danube. This development of the Greek marine, which threatened to take large proportions, excited the jealousy of England, and that power, under the Palmerston ministry in 1850, seizing a flimsy pretext of the stoning of the house of a Portuguese Jew, named Pacifico, by the street boys in Athens on Easter day, sent a powerful fleet under Admiral Parker to seek redress. They asked for a large indemnity and an apology from the Greek Government, claiming Pacifico as a British subject. On the refusal of the Greek Government to comply, the British admiral seized hundreds of Greek vessels and towed them to the Bay of Salamis. Most of them were loaded with perishable cargoes, and thus brought ruin to their owners. Greece had finally to yield.

By this time many enterprising Greeks had established themselves in the large commercial cities of Western Europe, as well as in Southern Russia, the lower Danube, Roumania, and Constantinople, and, having amassed great wealth, sent large sums to Greece from patriotic motives.

It is with these moneys chiefly that the National University of Athens, the Polytechnic School, the Observatory, the Sina Academy, the Arsakeion, orphan asylums, theological seminaries, national museum, and other public institutions were built. And while such progress was being made within the kingdom, Crete and the other islands were groaning under Turkish rule, Macedonia was overrun by Bulgarian emissaries and Roumanian agents to propagate Slav ideas, while in the other provinces of European Turkey and the eastern coast of Asia Minor thousands of Greeks were looking to Athens for protection from Turkish excesses.

Greece could not, cannot remain indifferent to these constant appeals of her children living without the kingdom. Many of these Greeks living abroad have their own kinsmen in Athens, men of importance, learning, and position. Their influence is felt by each successive government, which is thus obliged to protect those who are living in the Turkish dominions, deprived of the blessings of liberty; and this task imposes heavy burdens on the little kindgom out of all proportion to its limited resources, and it is chiefly to one of these circumstances that the recent disasters of Greece are due.

Crete, with a Christian population of two hundred and fifty thousand souls (the other fifty thousand are Mussulmans), rose in insurrection more than half a dozen times, since she was given back to Turkey in 1830, and every time that the movement was suppressed by Turkey, assisted openly or secretly by the European powers, the Sultan promised reforms and gave promises for the amelioration of the condition of the wretched inhabitants, which were never fulfilled. These periodical insurrections placed a very heavy burden on Greece, particularly those of 1866, 1876, and 1896, when the Greek Government had to feed more than sixty thousand Cretan refugees, mostly women and children, taxing its resources to the utmost extent.

The massacres of Christians at Canea in the fall of 1896 roused, very naturally, a cry of indignation all over Greece, and the people at large clamored for interference, accusing both king and government of cowardice and neglect of a sacred duty. The opposition joined forces with the popular movement, and the pressure to act became thus irresistible. A Greek squadron and a small contingent of the Greek army were despatched to Crete to protect the Christians. The sequel is well known. The great powers sent their fleets and an army of occupation to Crete, drove back the Greek vessels, bombarded the Christian positions, and established a strict blockade in order to reduce them to obedience by starvation. Equity, justice, and international law were ignored, or, to speak more plainly, were superseded by brute force, by might against right. The Christians did not lay down their arms, but Turkey, encouraged by at least one of the great powers, massed a large army of one hundred and fifty thousand on the Greek frontier, ostensibly under the command of Edhem Pacha, but practically conducted by German officers, with one hundred and fifty Krupp guns. Against this formidable force the Greeks under the Crown Prince could only oppose thirty-five thousand men, half of whom were raw recruits, full of enthusiasm it is true, but poorly drilled and half disciplined.

The result could be easily foreseen. The Greek army was defeated and forced to evacuate Thessaly, the German Emperor sent congratulatory telegrams to the Sultan, a heavy war indemnity and a curtailment of her frontiers were imposed on Greece, and a foreign control was established over her finances.

The diplomats of the great powers are now

rubbing their hands with satisfaction at having localized the war, prevented the reopening of the Eastern question, and pacified Crete. But have they really done so? Perfect chaos reigns now in Crete on account of the jealousy and the mistrust of the powers of each other. Half a dozen governors have been proposed and rejected. England wants a Battenberg, Russia a Montenegrin, Italy an Italian, Germany has her own candidate, and so forth. In the mean while the European fleets are at anchor at Canea and Heraclion, and their contingents occupy the four fortresses of the island, ostensibly to protect the Mussulmans from the attacks of the Christians. The latter have placed themselves at the disposal of the powers, who have done nothing to establish a local government, and it is very likely that this chaotic state of things will last for some time to come. A more ignominious failure than that of the powers trying to govern Crete can hardly be imagined.

History will register with shame these doings of the great powers at the end of the nineteenth century. Their conduct toward Greece has been cruel and inconsistent; but if the truth must be said, some of the powers have always tried to keep Greece backward for selfish purposes and for the accomplishment of their own designs. They are acting thus not from love for Turkey, but from hostility toward Greece. The Austrian men-of-war were about to bombard Mersina the other day, merely because some Turkish zaptiehs maltreated an Austrian subject. But when a whole Christian population of two hundred and fifty thousand souls in Crete were menaced with massacre, and some hundreds of them were actually butchered by the Turks at Canea, the powers found fault with Greece for sending men-of-war and soldiers for their protection. They evidently have different weights and measures for the small and large states. The application of this pernicious principle means assuredly the annihilation of the independence of the small states in favor of the large ones.

Nothing is heard any more about the promised reforms by the Sultan. The massacre of the Armenians seems forgotten. Abdul Hamid knows that the so-called concert of the powers is a sham and that they mistrust and are afraid of each other. He has succeeded in rendering the celebrated concert the laughing-stock of the civilized world. Turkey is safe, not because she is guarded by the Turkish army, but because she is supported by European bayonets. It is really a privileged position, which nobody understands better than the Sultan himself. If Greece has sinned, it was on the side of compassion for her oppressed children and coreligionists. She is bleeding from every pore of her mutilated body, but there is a Nemesis which sooner or later will overtake those who seem to rejoice now at her defeat and humiliation. There is, however, great vitality in the Greek race. Hellenism has gone through many severe trials in past ages and finally has come out victorious. It may be hoped that the Greeks of to-day will profit by the severe lessons which they have received, and their late disaster may after all prove a blessing in disguise, if they go bravely to work, reform their political system, pay more attention to interior improvements than to foreign politics, elevate the national character, and fulfil their national aspirations by the arts of peace, and attract once more the sympathies of those to whom the word "Hellas" means always civilization and progress.

CHRISTIAN GREECE AND LIVING GREEK.

CHAPTER I.

AN HISTORICAL SKETCH OF GREEK.*

WHEN I offered to read a paper this evening, it was my intention to speak on the new anatomical nomenclature offered by a German anatomical society. I not only had in view to concur with those who have already expressed themselves on this new lexicology, and who have said that the committee of anatomists who composed the work mentioned have *not* done what they claim. I wished to go a step farther and demonstrate in what way the committee could have fulfilled their promise—could have executed their intention.

As we know, the authors decided to give all words in one language—in Latin—and to construct them correctly. In reality most words

---

* Read before the German Medical Society of the city of New York, February 3d, 1896.

are, and it could not be otherwise, Latinized Greek, or they are hybrid words; in some of them, of more than two syllables, we find the syllables alternately from the one and the other language; and finally, as has been shown already, many words are grammatically incorrect.

Any one who gives a glance at this new nomenclature cannot fail to notice barbarisms in large numbers. In this copy which I pass around I have marked some on the first pages.

The anatomists have undertaken a thing which was an impossibility—namely, to develop further (*fortbilden*) a dead language, to treat a dead language as a living one.

Had the committee, however, taken the living Greek for a basis, had they made use of a modern Greek work on anatomy, had they consulted real Greeks, they would have fulfilled all their promises, executed all their intentions, without the arduous labor of seven years and the expenditure of quite a sum of money, as enumerated by them. Indeed, their arduous work would have been unnecessary if the lexicology of our Greek colleagues of to-day—the best imaginable—had been accepted.

To prove the superiority of this really homogeneous, faultless Greek nomenclature, I wrote to Athens for a modern Greek book on anatomy, since I could not find a copy in New York. The book arrived too late to enable me to complete my preparations, and therefore I selected another subject. Some of you will reproach me for occupying your time with a theme which may appear unusual in this place, but if it were not for this I should not regret the change, because, before we can understand the significance of the living Greek language as the one to be selected for our anatomy and for other practical purposes, we must come to an understanding of the language itself, and this can best be accomplished if we begin with the study of certain historical facts.

Some years ago the Greek question was introduced into the medical world by no less a person than Rudolf Virchow, in his inaugural address as rector of the Berlin University, on October 15th, 1892. While Virchow spoke of school Greek only, and did not mention living Greek at all, the credit is due to the *Medical Record* of having been the first to call our attention to living Greek. The impulse which was given by the editor of that journal has found an echo in the medical press; in all languages in all civilized countries has the subject been discussed; even in the scientific papers of German philologists has the question been considered. The Greek question has thus become a legitimate one for us, and, judging from the interest with which it has been treated, we may surely predict for it a brilliant future.

If we arrive at an understanding of the significance of the living Greek language, if we familiarize ourselves with certain facts concerning this idiom, we shall notice first of all that there exists much less a new Greek than there exists a new German. We shall find that the language which is spoken and written in Greece this very day is exactly two thousand three hundred years old. We shall find that the prevailing assertion that we do not know how the Greek was pronounced during the classical period is based upon an error. We shall find that the stones from the seventh century B.C., and from that time through all the centuries until the present one, speak to us and give us the pronunciation of each and every century.

We shall have to deal with many errors concerning the Greek language and the Greeks themselves, with errors which are as extensive almost as the whole civilized world and as old; some as old as the dissociation of the Latin from the Greek Church—that is, more than eight hundred years; others as old as the notorious *Dialogus Erasmi Roterdami de græci latinique pronunciatione*—namely, three hundred and sixty-eight years. With truth and simplicity alone can the errors concerning Greek be crushed.

To do justice to the subject, the time allowed for a simple lecture would be too short. It will be enough if I confine myself this evening to giving a sketch of the historical development of the modern Greek language.

My remarks are based not only on the researches of prominent native Greek philologists— I wish to mention especially Hatzidakis[*] who, like many learned Greeks, has made his studies of old Greek philology in German universities, and who with pride calls himself a scholar of Delbrück; and the great scholar, Papadimitrakopulos, whose crushing arguments, as my esteemed friend Professor Leotsakos expresses himself, are not less formidable in strength and length than his name—but also the writings of different authors of different countries found in the periodical Ἑλλάς, published by the Philhellenic Society of Amsterdam, and other periodicals and books.

[*] In this paper I avail myself mostly of the book of G. N. Hatzidakis, "Einleitung in die neugriechische Grammatik," Leipzig, 1892.

It is impossible reasonably to dispute the fact that the Greek language of to-day is an uninterrupted continuation of ancient Greek. The living Greek of to-day shows much less deviation from the Greek of two thousand and more years ago than any other European language shows in the course of centuries.

In the great days of Greece, when its literary works received the applause and admiration of enlightened scholars, authors took great pains to write well, fearing that they might be despised or forgotten. This emulation produced great works. The language was at its greatest perfection. Every writer found the beautiful form for his thoughts and for the expression of his ideas. Inevitable vicissitudes, in the first instance of civil dissensions, have gradually led to decadence. Literature received less and less serious attention. Poetry was first to decline. Orators and historians were replaced by speakers and chroniclers. Polybius, the historian (204–122 B.C.), complained of the difficulty he had of putting a nice thought into equally nice form, and he asks his readers not to pay so much attention to the form as to the contents of his writings. Such a request could never have been made by Thucydides or Demosthenes. The land of heroes, of liberty, came under bondage, and the powerful and creative spirit of the old Greeks weakened.

The history of the Greek language is the mirror of the history of the Greek nation. Naturally enough, a depressed and suppressed nation cannot create national works. Patriotism, national pride, free political life, and religion are necessary to inspire the creation of great monuments of literature. While the later Greeks, however, could no longer write classically, they retained a keen sense for the beauties of the classical language. Instead of creating new works themselves, they became imitators of the old writers, scrupulous imitators of their words and forms.

All nations have more or less a double language; nowhere do the illiterate use the same forms and words as the educated; even the latter use only exceptionally artistic and choice language. A well-marked diglossy has existed among the Greeks at all times.

When, after Alexander the Great, Greek had become the world and court language, a language for prose, the language for the educated class was created, the so-called κοινή, the general, and the foundations of this general language were the Attic writers; admixed were provincialisms.

The sources for the study of this language, the κοινή, are the writers of the Alexandrian period, above all the papyri and the numerous inscriptions which are found in all parts of Greece. This fine literary language, the κοινή, is yet the language of to-day; it is a finished language which has taken up to its completion words from the dialects, but which is independent of dialects. It is the centre around which the dialects are arranged.

Through two thousand years the Greek language has proved to be of a most remarkable terseness compared with the Romanic and the German languages; it is surprising how little Greek has changed in words as well as in forms. Most grammatical forms of the pure Attic are in use this very day. The difference between the new and the old consists principally in the simplification of old grammar; the new elements, forms, and construction in the new Greek are only exceptionally formed. This simplification, consisting in the generalizing of some and dropping of other elements, did not take place recently, but during the time of the establishment of the κοινή; it is therefore not a characteristic of the new Greek, but it appears more clearly and distinctly in it.

It has been said that the firmness and the tenacity of the character of the Greeks, who, more than any other subdued nation, remained true to their customs and habits, were the cause of their clinging to their language more than any other nation. But there exist other peoples with as much tenacity of character as the Greeks who also have preserved their customs and habits, who, however, did not preserve their language unchanged through all the centuries as did the Greeks. Greek of to-day is essentially old Attic Greek. By the Greeks the contemporaneous language of the different periods of Greece was never used instead of or confounded with the κοινή, any more than by the Romans during the fourth and fifth centuries of the Christian era would be used the Italian of their time, which was considered as being corrupt, instead of the classical Latin. At no time was there a contemporaneous general demotic language deviating much from the κοινή; if such a language, deviating as much as, for instance, French from Latin, ever had existed, there would be quite a different Greek literary language at present.

One of the most plausible reasons why the

Greek of to-day is essentially the Greek of the old glorious time, is the magnificence of the beauty and contents of the classical monuments of literature. As a large tree which excludes all sun rays underneath its mighty foliage will not permit other plants to be lighted and warmed and to thrive within its reach, so have the overwhelming magnitude and the sublimity of the classical form of the old literature prevented a post-classical literature from developing. Since the Greeks for centuries had, on the one hand, the richest and most beautiful works of the classical period, and, on the other hand, the most insignificant products of a later time, they naturally enough had recourse again and again to the old treasures. During the reign of barbarism in Europe—that is, from the fifth to the twelfth century—the Greeks were the exclusive, jealous conservators of science, arts, industry; they did not allow, even to themselves, that something of the sacred deposit be changed, as if during this sad gap in the history of Europe they had had the thought of transmitting all intact to more prosperous times. During the Latin and the Byzantine reign the Greek writers, neither controlled nor encouraged by public opinion, neglected themselves, and their style necessarily deteriorated. Books were not read, and every one wrote only for his own satisfaction. Because the beauties of the classicity of old could not be found in contemporaneous work the error was made of blaming the language for it.

It is easily understood that the writers of many centuries, even the less educated, who had nothing of the genius of their ancestors, in their admiration of the classical language retained most anxiously all the old orthography, the words, the modes of expression, the constructions, because all considered the old language as one of extreme beauty. They looked upon new elements which might be introduced into it as vulgar corruptions. Every writer had the intention to use the aristocratic, pure ideal language instead of the vulgar and irregular. Thus can be explained the fact that the schools, the church, the administration, the military, the legislature, the courts, the correspondents, and the *literati* of all kinds, during all the centuries while Greece was in bondage, used the archaic language. Books written in dialects, such, for instance, as A B C books or readers, grammars of contemporaneous Greek, were altogether unknown things at those times. In aristocratic society κοινή only was spoken. Even the Roman reign, which in the West had forced many nations to adopt the Latin, had not been able to interfere with the continuation and the cultivation of the Greek, for *Græcia capta ferum victorem cepit.* Rome itself was made a *græca urbs.*

The Roman Empire ceased to be. Other nations did not emigrate into Greece, at least not in large numbers. If there had been an invasion numerous enough, it would have left traces in the people's language; that is, in the dialects. The language of the continental part of Greece, however, remained as free from such foreign elements as did the language of the islands, of which it is known positively that they were not invaded by foreigners, especially southern Laconia and Maina, for instance. Besides, it is to be taken into consideration that the foreigners who did come before the thirteenth century did not come as conquerors, they were simply nomads, people without culture and relatively not numerous; they came among a nation of high culture. It stands to reason that they would adopt the Greek culture, religion, and language rather than that the Greeks would adopt anything of the kind from them.

An interruption of Greek culture and of the use of the pure, fine literary language has never happened in Greece, not even after the Latin conquest in 1204 and the Turkish in 1453. The Attic, the classical language, became, so to say, transfigured; its forms, words, constructions, expressions, orthography, were considered as something sacred, as something which alone had a right to existence.

Everybody will understand that all the above-named conditions were unfavorable to the creation of a new literary language and a new national literature. There remained on the one hand the antiquated literary language, and on the other hand the freely developed popular language—the dialects. Neither one could supply all demands. After the eleventh century the necessity was felt for the alteration of the former, the literary language, as it appeared antiquated. The adoption of a more modern phase, which would be more easily understood, was suggested. But then came the Frankish adventurers who conquered Constantinople, divided Greece among themselves, and brought the most terrific misery on the whole Greek world. While the political condition thus grew worse every day, there was a want of national spirit, which is the first essential for a national literature. It remained as it was; the treasures of the classical literature and the church were the only links which held all Greeks together.

Nothing has been more potent in the preservation of the old Greek than the influence of the church. During the dark night which covered the land while the Turks governed it, there remained, overlooked by the conquerors, two points still faintly illuminated by the departing sun rays of liberty: the church with some privileges granted for political reasons, and the inaccessible mountainous regions of old Hellas, where the bravest found refuge from bondage.

More than a hundred times a year, and for hours at a time, all Greeks had to hear in their churches the fine old Greek, and principally on this account a knowledge of the old Greek was preserved through all the centuries, even among the humblest people. People, although unable either to read or to write, understood the mass very well, the sermon—in short, everything they heard in church. They could be seen in olden times gathered together and listening attentively to one among them possessed of a certain amount of education acquired in a convent or elsewhere, explaining the difficult words or expressions.

It has been said, on the other hand, that the

very existence of the Orthodox Church has been the reason that living Greek was considered as a new language. The Byzantines, and the people depending on them, were completely separated from the western European nations in consequence of religious and political events. The fact is that the Byzantines, their heirs, and their descendants, even to this very day, do not consider themselves as belonging to Europe. We notice this in every newspaper and in daily conversation. When Greeks speak of Germans, French, and English, they name them, as in contrast to themselves, Europeans. The Orthodox Church forms a world of its own; it is a complex of nations and states, some of them half civilized, living between civilized Europe and barbaric Asia. This multiform composition of nations, which in the past has been the bulwark against Asiatic barbarism, seems to be destined for the future to be the medium of bringing civilization from Europe into Asia. Up to date it has been little known, but much misrepresented. This seclusion has been the impediment to the scientific study of the middle and new Greek.

In consequence of the separation of the Occidental from the Oriental church—that is, the Orthodox from the Roman Catholic—the history of the Greeks during the Byzantine era has been neglected by the schools in Western Europe. The hostility toward the Orthodox Church was extended to the Greeks and the living Greek language. Thus we see that the church on the one hand helped to preserve the old Greek language, and, on the other hand, was indirectly the cause that living Greek was condemned, despised, calumniated. The world is full of wrong and misery caused by religious dissension.

It is about time that our schools turned their attention to the history of Byzantine Greece. While German, French, English, Italian, and Spanish history are treated with due consideration, Byzantine history is restricted to a few paragraphs only, and these so brief that no satisfactory understanding is possible.

The close relation of the middle Greek language with the old Greek is evident. There is hardly any branch of classical philology which is not enlightened by the study of the Byzantines. Even the vulgar Greek, the dialects, and the dialects severally, as we shall see later on, have proved to be essential and important parts of the history of the Greek language. This has been fully demonstrated by a number of Greek philologists, by Maurophrydcs, Deffner, S. Meyer, Foy, Dossios, Hatzidakis, Psichari, Oekonomides, Thumb, and others.

No contemporaneous language had any literature except in the songs of the Klephts. In the ravines of the Pindus, of the Olympus, of the Aroanias, and of the Peloponnesus the fearless men who raised the name Klepht to a pinnacle of honor, with a certain pride developed by their bravery, sang their Klepht songs while constantly under arms, and fighting incessantly to guard their independence. These songs are simple and artless, but often sublime, as the summits of the mountains that they came from, and of the same natural beauty as the wild flowers which likewise rooted there.

The Klephts were a robust people, but all their poetry is characterized by a spirit of chastity, though sad and melancholy as was their history. The poets are anonymous, like the heroes of those times. Here are some examples of Klepht songs:

"I will join the Klephts to become the pride of the desert and the dweller of the forest. I will live in the mountains and on their summits, live where the wild beasts have their lair. I may have the rocks for my couch and the snow for my cover, but I will not serve the Turks."

As in the poems of Homer the horses of Achilles and the rivers of Troy assume the human voice; as in the old mythology every tree, every grotto, every spring is animated by a nymph dwelling within, so in these songs are the woods, the eagles perching on the summits of the rocks, the mountains themselves, the sun and the moon, the rivers and the soil and the clouds of heaven made to speak, narrating the adventures of the Klephts, lamenting their death, consoling their mothers and all their grief-stricken family. Touching all chords, the most tender, the most sublime, they give an account of the events of family life and of the life in the fields; exactly like the ancient rhapsodies they draw a picture of the Greek people and their political history during a period which is not otherwise recorded.

In one of the songs a dying Klepht dictates his last will: "Dig a grave for me, large and deep that I may stand upright with my gun ready to fight. Open also a window to the right that the swallows may come to announce the springtime, and that the nightingale may come to sing of May blossom."

A mother whose son has been killed expresses her grief: "The harts and the deers run on the mountains, only one sad roe does not follow them; she seeks the shade and rests on her left side; when she finds clear water she disturbs it before drinking. The sun meets her, rests on her way and asks: What aileth thee, my poor roe? Why dost thou seek the shade and rest on thy left side? Sun, thou askest me, and I will answer thee. For twelve years I was childless; finally I had one child. I nourished and I raised it. When it was exactly two years old a hunter killed it. Malediction upon thee, hunter, thou hast killed my husband and thou hast robbed me of my child."

In many of these songs we observe all the vivacity of the inexhaustible imagination of the ancients, and we are carried away into the remote times when poetical creations peopled the Olympus and when the poets made them enter into human dramas.

It was in Athens last summer; the moon shone, the stars were more brilliant than we see them in our climate, all surroundings were as beautiful as we can find them only in the most favored spots of our planet, when I heard for the first time a Klepht song, sung by some sons of the mountains who were passing by. I was spellbound, and it seemed to me as if these voices which I heard and the sympathetic expression of the words, when compared with the songs heard from artists at an opera, were as much more genuine as the surrounding nature was superior to the painted scenery of the stage. The song I listened to was the following: "Why are the mountains dark and threatening? Is it because the wind shakes them, because the rain strikes them? It is not the wind that shakes them, it is not the rain that pours down; it is Charon (death) passing with the dead. He chases the young before him, the old are forced to follow him, and the children of tender age he has grouped on his saddle. (There being no rivers in the mountains, the Klepht poets have represented Charon as a horseman.) The aged beg of him, the young fall on their knees before him: Stay, O death, near a village, stay near a fresh spring, that the old may quench their thirst, that the young may throw the stone (disk), and that the children may gather flowers. I shall not rest at a village nor stay at a fresh spring. The mothers would come to fetch water and would meet their children. the spouses would find themselves and I could not separate them again."

Many a beautiful night I spent at the Phaleron with a dear Greek friend, a grave man of science. He recited for me many of the Klepht songs; one of those I liked the best was a ballad, and when I heard it I said at once, Bürger must have borrowed from it for his best poem, "Leonore." It was as follows:

"O mother with thy nine sons and thy only daughter, thy beloved daughter is tenderly caressed. She was twelve years old and the sun had not seen her yet. Thou bathest her, and thou braidest her hair in the shade of the night, and thou fastenest the hair with ribbons under the rays of the evening star or the morning star. She is asked to marry in a foreign land, quite far away, in Babylonia. Her eight brothers refuse their consent, but Constantine consents: Give her, O my mother, send Arete into the foreign land, that I may find consolation whenever I shall travel far away, and there may be a roof under which I can repose. Thou art prudent, Constantine, but what thou sayest is not wise. And when, O my son, sickness or death should happen to us, who will bring her to me? He gave God for bond and called the saints as witnesses that if death or sickness should happen, if joy or sorrow should befall them, he would go to fetch her. Then came a year of misfortune, a month of distress. The pest raged and took away the nine sons. The mother alone was left, a reed in the midst of the desert. Before eight graves she struck her chest, from the grave of Constantine she had the stone raised. Rise, O my Constantine, I will have my Arete. Thou hast given God for bond and the saints for witnesses, that when joy or grief should happen thou wouldst go to fetch her. This adjuration brought him from his tomb. Out of a cloud he made a horse for himself, and out of a star a bridle, he had the moon for companion and went to fetch his sister. He traversed the mountain ranges and he found her combing her hair in the moonshine. He saluted her from the distance, saying: Come with me, my sister, our mother calls thee to her side. Ah, my brother, at what unusual hour thou callest on me. If it is joy which is waiting for me, let me know it that I may put on my garments embroidered with gold; if thou grievest for a sad event then I remain as I am. Come with me, my Arete, and remain as thou art. Along the road they went; they met little birds singing and saying: Who has ever seen a nice girl dragged away by a dead man? Do you understand, my dear Constantine, what the little birds are saying: Who has ever seen a nice girl dragged away by a dead man? They are unreasonable birds. Let them sing and say what they like. They continued their route, and other birds said again: What do we see! What a sad sight! the living travelling with the dead! Did you understand, my Constantine, what the birds were saying about the living travelling with the dead? They are birds; they have nothing else to do but to sing and to gossip. I fear thee, O my brother, thou hast the odor of incense. Last night we went to the chapel of St. John and the priest put much incense in his censer. They went on further and other birds said: God Almigthy, this is a great miracle which thou doest! A corpse drags after him a young girl full of beauty and of grace. Arete heard it and her heart broke. Did you understand, my Constantine, what the little birds said? Tell me where is thy beautiful hair, thy heavy beard? I have had a grave sickness which threatened to be fatal. It is on this account that I have lost my blond hair and my heavy beard. They found the house closed and the door latched. Cobwebs were spread over all the windows. Open, O my mother, open for me. I am your Arete. If thou art Charon, go on thy way. I have no more children to give thee. My poor Arete is far from here, she lives in a foreign land. Open, open, my mother. I am thy Constantine. I gave thee God for bond and the saints for witnesses that if joy or sadness should happen I would bring her to thee. Before she could reach the door her soul departed."

These few examples show that poetry did not die out in the land that was at one time so glorious. The germs still exist, and some day the rays of national prosperity may shine on Parnassus covered with a new flora.

May not the form of poetry of which the above are examples be the very same form of poetry that was current among the illiterate class of people in ancient times? This form of language has not been transmitted by the classical authors, but many of the words and grammatical types are of the remotest epoch. They have disappeared from literary language, but never from the language of the people.

Here is a world of study and one that would certainly prove more satisfactory to philologist and philological science than the constant fault-finding with modern Greek and so-called modern Greek pronunciation.

The different parts of Greece are widely scattered, being separated by the sea, by highlands, and by other nations intervening. This peculiarity of Greeks living secluded from Greeks became more marked politically when the provinces of the Byzantine reign were conquered. This was another reason why a new people's language would not develop and could not spread. A new national language understood by all Greeks did not exist. There were only the many dialects of the different provinces, and so we find in regard to the people's contemporaneous language polyglossy on the one hand and aglossy on the other. The language to which all the Greeks adhered was the virginal, immortal old Greek.

It is true that in Cyprus and Crete attempts were made for a while to write contemporaneous language, but these attempts were futile. Writers in the politically and geographically lacerated Greece wrote the idiom of their respective provinces. These dialects were too much intermixed with topical forms and expressions for the majority of the Greeks to understand them, and so none of these writings laid a foundation for a new literary language of the whole nation. Besides, all these writings are valueless; they show no trace of genuine national spirit and national character; they are poor imitations of weak foreign originals. The difficulty of raising the contemporaneous language of Cyprus or Maina to the dignity of a national language became an impossibility with the conquest and political destruction of these two islands.

The Turkish reign brought along with many other evils much ignorance. This ignorance, one would assume, might have favored the abandonment of the old language. Indeed, the people's idioms were spoken during this fearful period, and attempts were made to use the vulgar language in literature, but more than ever in vain. The Roman Catholic priests, in order to make propaganda among the Greeks, used the vulgar language, and monks of this church have translated the liturgy into the contemporaneous idiom of the people, some of these translations being printed even in Latin characters; this same language they spoke in church. The Greeks always entertained a certain dislike toward the people's language, and are careful not to employ it when they speak of sacred things. In some cases it was the church which caused constructions or changes in the meaning of words. It is on this account that many words which otherwise would have been lost are preserved. Some such words became, so to say, sanctified, and the contemporaneous language, in order not to use these words for profane meaning, was obliged to supply corresponding ones. A Greek will not name, for instance, bread and wine, when spoken of as being used in church, by the names ψωμί and κρασί, which words are of the people's and not of the literary and the church language, like some others used when spoken of as sacred, παρθένος, the virgin, otherwise κορίτσι, κυρασιά. In addition to this aversion against popular language it came about that this despised language was spoken, and, of course, badly spoken, by men who themselves were much hated by the orthodox Greeks.

At the time when the Turks conquered Crete and had all Greece under their oppressive control, the Greeks commenced to contemplate how to regain their liberty and independence.

A factor in favor of the preservation of the pure literary language during the Turkish reign was that in all the Greek colonies, in Venice, in Moldavia and Wallachia, in Joannina, in Constantinople, in Smyrna, in Jerusalem, in Bucharest, everywhere numerous Greek schools were established and the old classical and new books were printed. All this kept up a most powerful enthusiasm for the old classical Greek everywhere. The old classics were studied with great zeal.

The Greeks inspired themselves by thoughts of the glory of Athens and Sparta. They felt it an insult to be called Ρωμαιός instead of Ἕλλην. Vessels destined to form in some future time the national navy were given patriotic names like Athena, Themistocles, Epaminondas. A strong old Greek love for liberty and independence developed in these generations. During a period of almost four centuries it kept the hearts of all Greeks inflamed, and culminated in deeds of heroism in the gigantic war for independence.

It could not be otherwise but that this united people, although united under Turkish bondage, should want one common language. One party, in boundless love for all that pertained to old Hellas, desired the language in which the history of the deeds of the old heroism, of the old love for liberty was transmitted; another party thought that such language was an impossibility, and wanted a modern language free from archaism as the best organ to educate and enlighten the people. This led to an excited linguistic war.

This war lasted long, and was carried on with much zeal and animosity, but it is all over now. The first party did not succeed because it fought against the spirit of the time, which did not approve of such a separation of the descendants from the ancestors, and because the language of its literary productions, written in various provincialisms not understood by all, could not possibly be accepted as the general idiom. The second party failed because the archaism which they wrote was not intelligible enough to the mass of the people.

Since neither of the two extremes succeeded, and neither the written nor the spoken tradition would suffice, a middle way was found and accepted; both forms were united, the one complementing the other; a mixture of old and new elements was established. This procedure was by no means new to the Greeks; it was planned by history itself. From its very inception the κοινή has not been used in its original purity; different concessions were made to the demands of the time—that is, a mixture of the old and the modern was formed. That such a mixture was nothing extraordinary or anything like a disturbing factor can be seen from the mixed language* of classical poets and from the prose of Xenophon. In making this mixture of old and new elements both were given the old forms. During the time of the Atticists and the Byzantines, as well as afterward and down to the present, the old elements were always considered as beautiful and noble; the new ones, however, as ugly and hurtful. The new elements were introduced for the sake of distinctness and convenience; the elegance was looked for in the old words. This middle way prescribed by history was to unite the Greeks, living, as we have seen, so to speak, in groups remote from each other, in the most satisfactory manner, even before the war of independence.

The origin of the Greek of to-day has been discussed a great deal. In the early part of this century some authors, especially Athanasios Christopulos, said that the new Greek was an Æolo-Doric dialect. This opinion has been criticised by Hatzidakis. He found that such assertion had no foundation. Although traces of Doric dialect could be found, the fundamental

---

* In speaking of mixed language in regard to Greek it is not meant to imply that Greek had any foreign elements. In this latter sense Greek was never a mixed language. The living Greek is the genuine daughter of the old Greek.

character was the κοινή. New Greek could not be called Æolo-Doric on account of the few Doric elements it contained.

The literary Greek of to-day consists of three elements:

1. Of Attic words, forms, and constructions which after the fall of Greece composed the simplified language, the κοινή, and of elements which, in conformity with the rules and laws of the language, have developed during the following centuries.

2. Of some words, forms, and constructions which during the classical time developed in the old dialects, which, however, entered into the Attic or into the κοινή, and thus formed a part of the entire κοινή.

3. Of some elements of old dialects which have not come with the κοινή, nor through the κοινή, but, on the contrary, independent from it, have been taken into the new Greek literary language.

How these elements were introduced into the κοινή is a question which would lead too far into philological study to be ventilated here. To enumerate examples of words and forms of old dialects thus introduced, words which are familiar to everybody, I will mention θάλασσα instead of θάλαττα, and the word ἀλέκτωρ, which was unknown in the Attic. The Athenians during the classical period did by no means speak the pure and fine Attic of Plato and Demosthenes; this can be shown by quotations from some old writers and also by inscriptions. It is most probable that some elements from old dialects have entered into the Attic and later on into the κοινή.

The literary Greek language of to-day owes its existence, in part at least, to the exertions of the great patriot Koraïs. Although the party of the καθαρισταί and the party of the χυδαϊσταί both stood up against Koraïs, the power of history, which was on Koraïs's side, was too strong for both parties, as we have seen.

Ἀδαμάντιος Κοραῆς was born April 27th, 1747, in Smyrna. From early youth he devoted himself to the study of old and new languages. In obedience to his father's wishes, he followed a mercantile career during the years 1772–78, without, however, neglecting the sciences. From 1782–88 he studied medicine in Montpellier and established himself as a practising physician in Paris. From there he worked incessantly for the education of his compatriots, and endeavored to awaken a favorable opinion of his nation in the Occidental countries. In 1800 he received the prize of the Academy for an edition of the writings of Hippocrates, but before this time he had attracted the attention of the world of learning by his ability. Later on he gained fame by his Greek translation of Beccaria's work on crimes and their punishments. This was followed by a work entitled "*De l'état actuel de la civilisation en Grèce*" (Paris, 1803). This was the first publication in Europe which gave true information on the intellectual and moral conditions of the new Greeks. During the period from 1805–27 he published a collection—twenty volumes—of old Greek classics, with critical explanations and prolegomena. In the latter he gave his patriotic teachings and advices. His greatest merit consisted in his promoting the Greek language; he eliminated as much as possible all foreign elements, but retained all that was good and useful from all centuries, rejecting the one-sided retention of the old words and forms as not compatible with the understanding of the people. He above all helped to establish a noble literary language. On account of his old age he could take no part in the rising of his fatherland in 1821, but aided it greatly by his patriotic pen. When Greece had gained her independence he took an active interest in the new formation of his country. In 1830–31 he attacked the government of Kapodistria in two publications. These books were in 1832 publicly destroyed on the stake in Nauplia by order of the brother of the president, Augustine Kapodistria. He died in 1833. His autobiography appeared in Paris in the same year.

As we have seen, Koraïs was still alive during the great national war. In the first year the necessity of draughting a constitution and of enacting legislation arose. Which language should be chosen? The contemporaneous people's language was not feasible, because it was as varied as possible; the Greeks as an entirety could not have understood it; besides, this people's language was poor and incapable of expressing ideas. The majority of the men composing the delegations were not teachers, or professors, or archæologists; they were physicians, sailors, merchants, priests, soldiers, and they used the mixed language sanctioned by practical use at that time. This language of the constitution and the legislation was the same as that in which the journals were written, in which the correspondence was kept. It was a time of activity, of great national impulse when this language was thus officially adopted, this language which had been predestined by history.

When Greece had regained her liberty after almost four centuries of Turkish bondage a regular government was to be erected. Countless numbers of demands were made on the language. A new life, a culture of which there had been no idea before, appeared suddenly before the Greeks. The language had to keep pace with the many new political, scientific, technical, commercial, journalistic requirements. Another nation would certainly under such circumstances simply have adopted with the foreign ideas the words also of foreign people, and would have formed a half-French and half-hybrid language. Not so the Greeks. Their history, their national pride, led them to exclude foreign words, led them to take the necessary elements from the old Greek to create new symbols for new ideas. This was a gigantic work. Stephanos Kumanudes has enumerated thirty thousand words which have been created during the last hundred years. Let us illustrate how the work was done by a few examples: During the eighteenth century the foreign word σταμπερία had been used to designate a printing establishment, then τυπογραφία had been formed, and from the latter a great many combinations were made which could not possibly have been formed from σταμπερία. In the same manner was ἀβουκάτος, then the genuine Greek δικηγόρος, or first πόστα, the ταχυδρομεῖον, etc. These and thousands of foreign words are now entirely out of use, and may be known only to the oldest people; the majority of the Greeks have no recollection of them. This process continues wherever a foreign word has been introduced. In my child's ἀλφαβητάριον I find the word μαϊμού (monkey). In vain should I look for it in a Greek dictionary. It is not a regular word adopted by the literary language. From μαϊμού we can form the diminutive μαϊμουδάκι, but that is all; while from the genuine and regular word πίθηκος I can form πιθηκίζω, πιθηκισμός, πιθηκιστής, etc. This shows how the metaphoric use of words like μαϊμού is very limited, that of πίθηκος, however, very extended. This facility of combinations which is so frequent is a great advantage in regard to genuine and regular Greek words.

Greek, the new literary language, has steadily become richer and more homogeneous ever since 1821; it undergoes changes all the time. Construction and forms are constantly remodelled after the old Greek, especially in those words and expressions which are taken from the old language; notwithstanding this the new Greek remains a mixed language. The remodelling is called purification. Incorrect elements, when discovered, are extirpated with more and more severity and tact. Greek has changed from age to age because it has continued to live; only what is dead, like Latin, does not change any more. The Greeks now possess a highly developed language; they can without much difficulty translate every thought expressed in foreign idiom into their mixed language, a thing which even Koraïs did not always succeed in. The Greeks of all parts can communicate with each other easily without the slightest fear of being misunderstood. Babylonian difficulties are an impossibility to-day. To what extent this language has spread we find when we consider the highly developed journalism, and the innumerable works which have been translated from other languages into Greek. Greek is the language of culture in the Orient.

By the establishment of this literary language quite remarkable advantages have been gained. Everything written by the Greeks of to-day can easily be understood by all those who have learned a little Greek in colleges in foreign lands. This could not be the case if some of the dialects had been adopted. The greatest of all advantages, the most important, is the marked similarity which exists between the literary language of to-day and the old Greek in regard to orthography and forms. For this reason the old Greek is not like a foreign language to the Greeks of to-day. How deplorable if it were otherwise, if the immortal treasures of the old literature were not their own! They would not be if another system, if the Latin alphabet, which was tried during the Frankish reign, had been adopted.

Let us once more take a look at the language question as it stood, and, as some will have it, as it stands perhaps among some querulous people to-day. There existed in Greece until the language question was firmly settled three parties:

1. The Purists or Atticists, καθαρισταί, or καθαρισταί τῆς γλώσσης, as Koraïs called them, who wish to carry purification to the extreme; they recognize only those words which are found in the old Greek literature as entitled to be accepted in new Greek. It is plausible to any one that not all words which really existed in the old Greek

language have been employed in literature, and besides, a considerable, say the largest, part of the literature which once existed in old Hellas has not come to us; thus these purists seem to place old Greek on the same footing with Latin.

2. Those who adhered, and adhere, to the literary language in use to-day.

3. Those who wished, and wish, for the vulgar Greek idiom; these are called the χυδαϊσταί.

That the Hyperatticists did not and will not succeed can be seen from history. Two thousand years ago Atticists, like Phrynichos, Mocris, and their disciples, were carrying on the same controversy; they wanted the same purification as the καθαρισταί of to-day, but in vain.

Prose, science, school, and press will uphold the literary language; poetry, especially the comical, will find its appropriate organ in the people's demotic (Klephtan songs, almanacs, comic journals) idiom. This will be as it was during the golden age of Greece, as is found in the chorus of the Attic tragedy and in lyric poetry.

Modern literary Greek, as history shows, is but Attic simplified and complemented.*

* A Greek translation of this lecture appeared in the Athenian journal Καιροί, June, 1896.

CHAPTER II.

THE PROPER PRONUNCIATION OF GREEK.*

ONE of the principal points in the study of a language is the knowledge and the application of its correct pronunciation. In order to learn the true pronunciation, one is obliged to go to the only rational and pure source, that is, to the people who speak the language; in the case of Greek, to the Greeks.

In the middle of the fifteenth century, after the fall of Constantinople, Greek fugitives came to all parts of Europe. The desire to do charity to these refugees without humiliating them too much on the one hand, and to take advantage of the opportunity offered to learn their language on the other, induced many persons to take Greek lessons from these Greeks. It became fashionable for every prince and every nobleman to have a Greek preceptor in his family. In every university a chair for Greek was established. This movement was similar to those taking place later on with reference to the

* Lecture delivered in Hossack Hall, Academy of Medicine, New York, June, 1896.

French language in Germany, England, Switzerland, and Holland when Frenchmen were forced to emigrate after the revocation of the Edict of Nantes, and later still, during the French Revolution.

With the introduction of the Greek language everywhere, Greek type was cast and editions of Greek authors were printed, most of them with learned notes and Latin translations. The students of the fifteenth and sixteenth centuries preferred to learn the language by means of translations rather than by the aid of the lexicon.

Europe had soon an immense number of Hellenists able to converse in the purest old Greek with their teachers, the Greeks from Constantinople, and later on the former became teachers themselves, surrounded by students. Among these Hellenists were Reuchlin, Melanchthon, Luther, and Erasmus.

All had, of course, the Byzantine pronunciation, which is essentially the same as that of the Greeks of to-day, and also that of the Attic orators.

With the end of the sixteenth century the pronunciation of Greek in the schools in the countries west of Greece became unsystematical, the language as it was then pronounced in the schools became unintelligible to the different peoples, and especially to the Greeks. This strange pronunciation owes its origin to the lucubrations of a scholar, and is in opposition to old and new traditions of the Greeks.

Dr. Edward Engel, in his book entitled: "Die Aussprache des Griechischen," has given the history, and in very plain words the definition of the school pronunciation of Greek. Many others before Engel, convinced that this pronunciation was incorrect and unscientific, had raised their voices; to Engel, however, is due the credit that his book made it impossible for any college professor to defend this school pronunciation as correct or justifiable, and learnedly to pull the wool over anybody's eyes. It is a curious fact that most of those men of profound learning who wrote for the school and against the true Greek pronunciation had absolutely no knowledge of the latter. Had they possessed such knowledge, and had they compared the pronunciation which the old inscriptions give with that of the living Greek of to-day, they could not have remained opposed to truth with a stubbornness which is incomprehensible.

This school pronunciation is an invention of Desiderius Erasmus, called Rotterdamus, and this invention he has described in his book, entitled, "De recta latini græcique sermonis pronunciatione dialogus," and printed in 1528.

There is a funny German story of a race between a hare and a pig, which commences as follows: "This story sounds like a lie; it must be true, however, otherwise we could not tell it." These words are a most appropriate introduction to the history of the Erasmian pronunciation. The history is true, the dialogue exists, this most absurd pronunciation has been transmitted from generation to generation down to the present day, that is, through three centuries.

When, as we have seen, after the conquest of Constantinople Greek scholars came to Western European countries and there gave lessons in the language of their ancestors, pupils did not doubt that their pronunciation had a historical right. Reuchlin, the great German philologist of the time of the Renaissance, had learned and taught the Greek language with the pronunciation of his Greek contemporaries, hence all persons who follow his example are called Reuchlinians. Even Erasmus himself spoke according to the Reuchlinian, but never in his life according to the method called after him;

he also taught his students the Reuchlinian pronunciation. Moreover, he requested his Greek friend Laskaris to furnish him a Greek teacher in order that his own children should learn the correct pronunciation. The fact that he spoke Reuchlinian can be established by quotations from one of his colloquies, where the following end rhymes are found: Echo rhymes: eruditionis —ὄνοις; episcopi—κόποι; ariolari—λάροι; astrologi —λόγοι; grammatiki—εἰκῇ; fameliki—λύκοι.

It was not until fifty or more years after Erasmus' death that the Erasmian pronunciation was adopted.

The above-mentioned dialogue "de recta pronunciatione" is indebted, as Engel narrates, according to well-authenticated tradition, to the following farce: Erasmus, who was childishly vain of his Latin and Greek knowledge, and who styled himself "the most amiable prince of science," met with the following adventure: A gay visitor from Paris, inclined to perpetrate all kinds of roguery, told him the following fib: He had made the acquaintance of some Greeks, very erudite men, who spoke in a manner entirely different from that in which all the world pronounced the Greek. And then he showed Erasmus how these remarkable Greeks spoke: exactly as if Greek were Dutch. Whether Erasmus put full or only partial faith in this story, it is certain he wished to use it in order to pamper his vanity; he intended to pose before the learned world as the inventor of this latest sagacity. Another version is that Erasmus himself intended a practical joke in writing this "dialogus de recta pronunciatione" and was amazed at being taken seriously by men of learning.

This dialogue, as already said, was composed in 1528. Most of the contestants in the battle about the Greek pronunciation have not even read this manifesto. It assumes the shape of a dialogue between a bear and a lion, and is exceedingly tedious, a feeble and attenuated waltz in trivial Latin.

The bear informed the lion that the old Greeks might have possessed the Dutch pronunciation, interspersed here and there with specimens of French expressions. This nonsense spread like a prairie fire. A flood of pamphlets agreeing with this dialogue was the result. *The professors of Greek need not boast of the history of their pronunciation of the Greek language; it shows anything but a scientific basis.* If any one doubts the truth of this statement, let him read the dialogue referred to; it can still be obtained. It is hardly necessary to marvel at this story. The dialogue was published at a time when, in spite of profound erudition, there was hardly an inkling of the substratum of a language, or even of the true relation of languages to each other, to be found in the world of learning; at a time when the greatest imaginable nonsense was uttered in an erudite manner. (Specimens in point are the Latin essays, comprising large volumes, concerning the question whether Adam was created with a navel.) At a large waste of learning, it was also proven at that period that Adam and Eve, before biting into the apple in Paradise, must have spoken Dutch, but after the fall, the French language.

As a diversion, let us take but a small sample of the comic ingenuousness from the dialogue:

"The lion asks: Quo sono credis haec veteres extulisse?

"Ursus: Referam quod in senatu grammaticorum audivi (namely, from the Parisian rogue).

"Leo: Sat erit.

"Ursus: Conjecturam faciebant ex linguis popularibus, in quibus utcunque corruptis resident antiquæ pronunciationis vestigia, oi diphthongus gallis quibusdam est familiarissima, quum vulgari more dicunt: mihi, tibi, sibi (moi, toi, soi); aut pronunciant fidem, legem ac regem (foi, loi, roi). Hic enim audis evidentur utramque vocalem o et i.

"Leo: Sic est profecto.

"Ursus: Ad eum prope modum sonuisse veteres arbitror μοί σοί, τοῖοι et κύριοι.

"Leo: Probabile narras." And so on.

The admirers of the great man of Rotterdam in different countries followed his system; they pronounced the Greek according to his instruction, or as if it were written in their own native tongue. The consequence was that since the sixteenth century a Babylonian confusion has prevailed concerning Greek pronunciation. Nobody understands the Greek of a foreigner, still less that of a Greek. The small boy, when he learned in his book of natural history that the whale belonged to the class of mammalia, remarked that the whale had brought disorder into zoölogy. Erasmus, indeed, is the whale in philology. It is impossible to say how much disorder this man has caused during the past three hundred and sixty-five years—that is, since he introduced his absurd pronunciation.

While it is amusing to read the origin of the Erasmian pronunciation, the matter presents also a very sad aspect. The introduction of the Erasmian absurdity was the death-blow to the knowledge of living Greek in Western Europe. Greek was only read, but no longer spoken since the Hellenists of the different countries Erasmized each in his own manner; the fearful cacophony of Erasmus took away the charms except those which were left for the deaf and dumb. But even though the Greek existed only for the eye, for the deaf and dumb, it was still beautiful; even the Erasmian pronunciation did not prevent its being studied and its literature read. Still, it is remarkable that the perfectly arbitrary, senseless invention of a cranky pedant should have remained in force these three centuries. The attempts to justify it, composing a bulky literature, dating back to 1528, are all based on sophistry.

While Englishmen and Frenchmen confessed that this pronunciation of Greek was really incorrect, and that they kept it up for convenience' sake, there were until recently Germans who mounted the high horse and persuaded themselves and their pupils that the Erasmian pronunciation was really the correct one. They took pains to invent scientific proofs of the correctness of the Erasmian method.

Whoever believes that such learned men did not exist in our times need only read a profoundly learned book, written by Friedrich Blass, entitled: "Ueber die Aussprache des Griechischen." Berlin: Weidmann, 3 Aufl., 1888.

A prince once offered a prize for an essay on the question: Why were the tails of fishes longer in winter than in summer; and great academicians of his country presented the most convincing proofs from Pliny, Galen, and other sources in support of this fish-tail question. Friedrich Blass with his book can well be compared with these academicians; his proofs of the correctness of the Erasmian pronunciation were as ridiculous as were those that fish-tails were longer in winter than in summer. Engel quotes some drastic passages from Blass' work, and criticises them severely. It cannot be the plan of this paper to enter into details; whoever wishes to study this question, although Erasmus is at last dead now, will find enough material in Engel's book, and still more in the more elaborate work of Papadimitracopoulos: Βάσανος τῶν περὶ τῆς ἑλληνικῆς προφορᾶς ἐρασμικῶν ἀποδείξεων. Athens: 1889, 752 pages. Engel compares Blass with Molière's Sganarelle. The quack Sganarelle palms himself off as a physician and explains to the father of a young lady who is dumb the cause of her infirmity.

"Sganarelle: The dumbness is caused by the loss of speech.

"Géronte: Very well. But please tell me what caused the loss of her speech?

"Sganarelle: All our best authorities will tell you that the cause is to be found in a cessation of the action of the tongue.

"Géronte: Yes, but how do you think did this cessation originate?

"Sganarelle: Aristotle says very interesting things on this subject.

"Géronte: I presume so.

"Sganarelle: Oh, that was a great man!

"Géronte: No doubt.

"Sganarelle: Do you understand Latin?

"Géronte: Not a word.

"Sganarelle (suddenly jumping up): You do not understand Latin? Cabricias arci thuram, catalamus, singulariter, nominativo, haec musa, bonus, bona, bonum.

"Jacquelin (the servant girl): Ah, what a smart man!"

The lucubrations of Prof. Friedrich Blass, embodied in the above-named book, have been completely refuted by Papadimitracopoulos. His book is the most exhaustive ever written on Greek pronunciation.

It is true German philologists have at last acknowledged—thanks to the just and severe criticism of men like Papadimitracopoulos—that the Erasmian pronunciation is faulty. They have ceased to dispute about Erasmian and Reuchlinian methods; they study instead with admirable zeal the inscriptions and establish the times at which the pronunciation of the different written sounds were transformed into the pronunciation of the Greeks of to-day. They found that there has been no material change these two thousand years. Despite the fact that the stones tell the exact truth unmistakably, as we shall see presently, how Greek was pronounced in every century ever since the seventh before Christ; despite the fact that the German schoolmasters, as well as the archæologists of all other countries, read this conclusive evidence about the only correct Greek pronunciation—this story sounds like a lie, but it must be true, otherwise it could not be told—they retain to this very day the Erasmian pronunciation in their schools, and many other schools in other countries do likewise.

Allow me now to read a letter which I received recently from a professor of Greek of one of our colleges, a man who has written a treatise on the teaching of the classical languages. This letter will illustrate what arguments some of our professors of Greek produce to suppress historical truth.

MARCH 9TH, 1896.

MY DEAR SIR:

You sent me a letter addressed to —— during my absence in Europe. I was away two years. I regret that in consequence of confusion among my papers, my answer has been delayed until this time.

I am not able to put my hand on the pamphlet to which you refer in your letter. Indeed, I am not sure that the copy which you sent to me ever reached me. But, nevertheless, I have learnt through conversation with others the subject of your thesis.

This whole matter is one of extreme difficulty. If Erasmus had never written his celebrated dialogue, the movement which Reuchlin had begun in Germany would have spread, I have no doubt, over the rest of Europe.* At the present time the Erasmian pronunciation so called has securely established itself. The difficulty of introducing the modern Greek pronunciation,

---

* I beg to say that Reuchlin did not commence a movement, but simply adhered to the only correct pronunciation.

either among physicians or in schools, is very great. I believe myself that we should all be better off if the modern Greek pronunciation had early been adopted and had always been used among scholars. *I do not believe for a moment that the modern Greek pronunciation represents the ancient practice*, but the practical advantages of using it seem to me to be very great, although I have a less high view of the modern Greeks and their language than I had before my recent residence in Athens of eight months. There is absolutely no modern literature worthy of the name. I find in conversation with my colleagues and other professional friends, a very fierce objection to disturbing the established practice. *I have no doubt that Blass' very extraordinary book, which has been translated into English by W. J. Purton, under the title,* "*Pronunciation of Ancient Greek*," and is published by Macmillan & Co., New York, has done much to strengthen the faith of those who believe that we ought not to adopt in schools the modern Greek practice.

It would be most unfortunate to provoke a discussion which led to nothing other than a hot division of opinion. We Greeks must not set to quarrelling among ourselves. We have difficulty enough at the present time to maintain ourselves in a community, a large part of which does not know what is best for itself.

With renewed expression of regret that my

answer to your letter should have been so long deferred, I remain,

Very truly yours.

I wish to add to this letter a few remarks which do not exactly concern the Greek pronunciation, but the calumniation of the living Greek, which is the manifestation of a conspiracy of ignorance and malevolence against Greece. Just such men who have travelled a little in Greece write in a vein peculiar to many tourists in general; they delight in exaggerations of exceptional and accidental incidents, and generalize from them. Thus, an Englishman writes that he finds in the modern Greek stereotyped phrases most distasteful to the scholar. Sure enough he could have found such phrases at home and everywhere. Everywhere scholarly speaking and writing is the exception, the commonplace is the rule. That wise Mirza truthfully has said: "I will praise God that not all men are wise, because if they were, wisdom would be too cheap."

German residents of Athens have sent a petition to Emperor William of Germany requesting to have the living Greek pronunciation adopted in the German schools. The petitioners say that the Erasmian pronunciation is an arbitrary one, by no means agreeing with the one which had existed during the classical period of Hellas. They further say that the literary language of the Greeks of to-day is almost equal to the old Greek. Every German student who has passed through the gymnasium is able, without further preparation, to understand modern Greek works, yet he cannot pronounce correctly the living Greek. For members of the German archæological institution, for instance, it is very painful to have to learn over again, on coming to Athens, the Greek language, the language to the study of which they had devoted many years of assiduous labor, for the reason that they had been taught at school the Erasmian pronunciation which deviates entirely from the pronunciation of the living Greek. The document then enters on the pronunciation of the different written sounds. Finally, it is pointed out that the Erasmian pronunciation has been already abandoned in the colleges of Italy, Belgium, Holland, England (they might have added, last but not least, America), and that it is high time that Germany should have done with the Erasmian tradition.

The Emperor of Germany has lost this opportunity to earn the praise and the thanks of coming generations, and has left this to the French Government, which has now, recognizing historical truth, decided to introduce the living Greek pronunciation into all the schools of the French republic.

This petition of German residents to the Emperor is not in harmony with the dignity of the science of philology. Since the German philologists are convinced that the Erasmian pronunciation is wrong, they must not teach it any longer. Schools which pretend to give scientific instruction should not teach something which confessedly is unscientific and false. As a rule they do not do so; they do not teach other living languages with an invented pronunciation. In regard to really dead languages, such as Hebrew and Latin, all schools in the world, with the exception of some English, follow a pronunciation which is based on tradition: for Hebrew, through the Portuguese Jews; for Latin, through the Italians. Only with Greek, schools make an exception. As to Greek, the existence of a pronunciation, the correctness of which can be traced through exactly twenty-six hundred years, should be the greatest inducement to bring the school instruction in close relation to practical life, so that the students could make practical use of the language. Unfortunately, schoolmasters are opposed to this view, their argument being: *non vitæ, sed scholæ discimus!*

Engel says: "The corner-stone of the Erasmian pronunciation is the idea 'it exists,' that is, state and city pay us to teach it. Some day when a minister of instruction orders it, we shall teach another pronunciation, and shall, when ordered to do so, prove that this new one and no other is correct." Such state of things is not creditable to the philologists. There can be no doubt that, as it is practicable and as soon as the professors have familiarized themselves with living Greek, Erasmian pronunciation will no longer be taught in any school.

When Greeks hear the Erasmian pronunciation of their language they cannot help laughing. Doctor Engel, while travelling in Greece, one day visited a school, and was delighted to observe with how much facility the boys read Demosthenes and Homer. He himself was asked to read before the class some Greek verses with the pronunciation as employed in German colleges. The Greek boys, while he was reading from the Iliad, did not know what to say at first, as they were under the impression he was reading German; but when they were given to understand that it should represent Greek, they burst into laughter, stamping with their feet, screaming and uttering cat-calls, and the principal himself could not help joining in the general hilarity. Any one can try the experiment of creating fun among Greeks by speaking to them of Erasmus of Rotterdam.

We can easily understand this hilarity when we learn how a Frenchman, who had long studied English and was thoroughly conversant with the literature, but had never become familiar with the sound of the language, read Tennyson's "Claribel":

> "At ev ze little bommess
> Az vart ze zeenet lon,
> At none ze veld be ommess
> Aboot ze most oldston
> At meednees ze mon commess
> An lokes doon alon
> Ere songz ze lint veet svelless
> Ze clirvoiced mari dvelless
> Ze slombvoos var ootvelless
> Ze babblang ronnel creepess
> Ze ollor grot replee—ess
> Vere Claribel lovelee—ess."

Nobody has ever asserted that Greek pronunciation has remained unchanged from the time of Kadmus until now. This would be a unique phenomenon. In the course of time the pronunciation of every language changes in correspondence to the change in the language itself. It is not probable that the pronunciation has changed during the same space of time more than the language itself. Classic Greek was a well-sounding language; we know this through the Greeks themselves, as well as through the Romans. The Greek of to-day still belongs to the most melodious of languages, its pronunciation gives a beautiful and pure harmony.

In the foregoing remarks on the pronunciation of Greek enough has been said to convince us that a reform of instruction in regard to pronunciation is an absolute necessity. In former times, before steam and electricity facilitated travelling, scholars might have given as an excuse for this wrong pronunciation, which could not serve in personal intercourse with Greeks, that they did not expect to meet Greeks. If this could have been an excuse once, it cannot serve as such any longer. The number of archæologists and philologists who visit Greece is increasing all the time. The opportunity to learn the living Greek should not be denied even to those who cannot enjoy the good fortune to visit Greece. There is no reason why the beautiful Greek language should be tortured hereafter in the Erasmian fashion. *It is to be hoped that now, when the inscriptions can be studied by anybody, when the history of Greece and of its entire language is better known, when there can be no more learned defence of Erasmian pronunciation, this pronunciation will be considered, as it should be, a monstrosity.* It is high time that our learning and studying youth be saved the useless torture of the mind, their parents the useless expense, and citizens generally the unnecessary taxation for schools teaching unscientific pronunciation.

Modern or living Greek, the literary language understood by all Greeks of to-day, is but Attic simplified and complemented by additional elements taken from the old dialects or formed in strict conformity with the old forms. Neither the language nor the pronunciation has changed materially these two thousand years. We have conclusive evidence from history that the language did not, and why it did not change. From the inscriptions, which, as a rule, were spelled phonetically, we know exactly how Greek was pronounced in all the centuries since the seventh B.C. The orthographic errors, the bad spelling found on inscriptions and in handwritings of the Greeks from the time of the seventh century B.C. through all the centuries are an excellent means of showing us how the different written sounds were pronounced in different centuries. The result of the study of the inscriptions has given conclusive evidence that the peculiarity of the pronunciation of the Greek vowels can be traced back as far at least as the fourth century B.C.

The accentuation is one of the great beauties of the Greek language, and the rules bearing upon it have been considered as sacred, and have not been changed these two thousand years. Accentuation is first mentioned in Plato's Kratylos (399 B.C.), where he says: "Often we change the accent, and instead of the acute we pronounce the grave." Πολλάκις τὰς ὀξύτητας μεταβάλλομεν, καὶ ἀντὶ ὀξείας βαρεῖαν ἐφθεγξάμεθα.

Demosthenes, in his oration Περὶ στεφάνου called Æschines a μισθωτόν, but had accentuated the word erroneously, namely, μίσθωτον, whereupon the audience corrected him by crying μισθωτόν.

The people of Athens in those times had a perfect knowledge of correct accentuation, although no signs for it were then in use. Everybody knew how his native tongue had to be accentuated.

It is generally conceded that Aristophanes, in the second half of the third century B.C., invented the accents, but closer research has shown that even in the time of Aristotle (fourth century B.C.) some manuscripts were accentuated. Thus, Aristophanes was not the inventor of accentuation, merely the one who introduced it. His disciple, Aristarch, in the middle of the second century B.C., wrote explicit rules to be observed in written accentuation.

It is established that even at the time of Aristotle the spiritus asper (ἡ δασεῖα) was no longer pronounced; that it existed only in writing, and ever since it has not been pronounced except by the Erasmians. No Greek, unless he has learned other languages, has any idea of our "h." Wherever it occurs in a foreign name, as, for instance, the German Hans, he writes not ἇνς, but Χάνς.

Writers on the accentuation of the Greek language are known from nearly all centuries, from the third B.C. to the seventh of the Christian era, from the ninth and tenth, from the twelfth, and all the following, up to our own. In all the works of such authors of these two thousand years, the rules of accentuation, the rules which the Greeks have observed from generation to generation, are given. The Greeks of to-day and of all the intervening times accentuate the words in the literary language the same as did their ancestors of the classical period. It is a misrepresentation, one of the inventions of some followers of Erasmus, to say that the Greeks of to-day have lost the old accentuation. If such were the case, would it not be probable that the change would have differed in various parts of Greece; if, for instance, the accentuation had been corrupted through the invasion of the Romans, Huns, Avanes, Slavs, Franks, and Turks? Manifold accentuation, however, never has existed; the educated Greeks of to-day, wherever they live, in all parts of the world, pronounce the words of their language according to rules which have stood the test of two thousand years. The Erasmian assertion of the loss of the old accentuation is one of those misstatements which contain a particle of truth and are therefore the more dangerous, the more deceiving. It is true that some words in the irregular, the people's, language are accentuated differently; but this is nothing new. Similar deviations existed in the oldest times. Thus, even the people's language has made no change in this regard.

At the time of Demosthenes, words in prose were pronounced according to accentuation, not according to metric quality. That such was also the case prior to Demosthenes' day can be shown by Hephastio, who says of the comic actors that they, in imitating life, spoke according to accentuation, not metrically τὸν γὰρ βίον οὗτοι μιμούμενοι θέλουσι διαλελυμένως διαλέγειν, καί μὴ ἐμμέτρως. If, then, the comic actors, in imitation of every-day life, did speak verses—poetry—as people spoke in every-day life, it is evident that people did not speak metrically, but according to accentuation, as they do to-day.

Of late we have had two societies of learned and prominent men who have worked with great zeal for the encouragement of the study of the living Greek with a view to have it adopted as the universal language of scholars. The first of these societies was founded by Gustave d'Eichthal, a Philhellenist with the zeal and soul of Byron, in the year 1867, for the study and practical use of Greek in France. The transactions and the other publications of the members of this society were collected in Gustave d'Eichthal's work, printed in Paris in 1887. Among the members were the Marquis de Saint-Hilaire, M. Renieri, Nefftzer, Fr. Dübner, A. Campeaux, E. Littré, Ch. Mendelssohn-Bartholdi, Robert Blackie, I. N. Valettas, Baudry, Louis Mallet, Basiadis, and last but not least, D. Bikelas.

Whatever could be said in elegant form in favor of Greek as the best international language for scholars, has been said and written by these eminent men of learning, by men who were accomplished scholars, both of classical and living Greek.

Gustave d'Eichthal died April 9th, 1886, at Paris. He had not seen the result of his unselfish labors, which he had longed for so ardently. Greek had not yet become the universal language. The valiant leaders of the Greek movement were admired, but although there had been official recognition and approval by the French Minister of Instruction of the aims of Gustave d'Eichthal and his co-laborers, no practical progress had been accomplished. Meanwhile a German, August Boltz, had published a book, entitled "Greek the General Language of the Future for Scholars," which infused new life into the question of the study of living Greek, and in the year 1886 another German, Dr. Eduard Engel, whom I have quoted extensively in this paper, commenced to write against the methods of instruction in Greek prevailing in German schools. In most powerful style he exposed the old fogyism, and a new movement in favor of living Greek followed. In the year

1889 an international Philhellenic society was called into existence in Amsterdam, and men of the highest ranks of life, princes who had distinguished themselves as Greek scholars, celebrated writers, men of learning from all parts of the civilized world became members to the number of five hundred. This body of Philhellenists published a quarterly review entitled 'Ελλάς, for the propagation of the ideas of the society. The articles published in this organ treat on philological studies, on the solution of the question of the true pronunciation, and give encouragement to the study of the living Greek in order that it may serve as an international language. The idea to make Greek the universal language of scholars will remain the order of the day and will be realized sooner or later.

Thus far the outcome of the noble labors of d'Eichthal and his followers has been the introduction of living Greek pronunciation in the French schools. As soon as this act of the Government had been proclaimed, I received many letters from my Greek friends in Paris and in Athens. One of them was from Professor Spiridis, who had been most active among those who had written and spoken to bring about this happy result. He wrote to me under date of March

27th, 1896, from Athens: "Dear Doctor:—The endless debates on the pronunciation of Greek in the French schools are closed, and the historical truth has at last triumphed. The old prejudices have all vanished. We are victorious. Other people will follow the lead of France." In Princeton University there is an earnest advocate of the true pronunciation of the Greek as a living language. Besides Princeton, we have a number of other colleges in this country in which Greek is taught as a living language with its true pronunciation: namely, MacAlester College, St. Paul, Minn.; Western University, Wooster, Ohio; the University of Colorado, Boulder, Col.; Emory College, Oxford, Ga.; Colby University, Waterville, Me.; Cornell University, Ithaca, N. Y.; Swarthmore College, Swarthmore, Pa.

The living Greek is a language remarkable in every respect. There is nothing wanting to constitute it the most beautiful language of Europe. It is, without the shadow of a doubt, the most perfect. Greece has excellent writers at the present time, although it is only three-quarters of a century since she became again a free and independent nation. There exists a large number of poets since the national resurrection, and there are a genius and creative power in their productions which foreign critics have not yet detected, owing to the comparatively insufficient knowledge of modern Greek. Lyricism is the chief characteristic of that poetry, but Alexander Rangabes and his son Kleon wrote besides very good dramas. The poems of Athanasias Christopoulos compare favorably with Anacreon's. Political satire is successfully employed in poetry by Alexander Soutsos, while the poetry of Dimitri Paparegopoulos and Spiridion Vassiliades is remarkable for its social aspirations and affinity with the genius of Euripides. Elias Tantalides, an exquisite singer of natural beauty, though blind, and George Zaloskostas, an artist in love lyrics, are very popular, while the poetry of Vizyenos shows many of the undefined longings of Shelley. Dionysius Solomos' celebrated "Ode to Liberty" has been translated into most languages. Aristoteles Valaoritis is known for his almost Æschylan solemnity. George Joures, the most remarkable of contemporary Greeks, is a second Aristophanes, with a strong Shakespearian vein, and shows considerable resemblance to Chaucer's tenderness of disposition. The most popular of all Greek writers of the present day, a historian and a poet, is Dimitrius Bikelas. His "Loukis Larras" is one of the best novels of our time, and has been printed in elegant editions and translated into many languages. Next to this masterpiece are his stories, known and translated into several languages. D. Bikelas translated several of Shakespeare's dramas into Greek in a masterly manner. His translation of Andersen's Fairy Tales is so beautiful that we are in doubt in which form we like it better—in the original or in this Greek translation.

The glory and prosperity of Greece are things of the future, not alone of the past. They are to come in the ordinary course of events, and not by the vain attempt of a return to the past.

The beautiful, like the Greek language, is like sunshine upon this world: the beautiful lives forever!

REMARKS AT THE LECTURE OF DR. A. ROSE. BY PROF. S. STANHOPE ORRIS, PRINCETON UNIVERSITY

A few years ago, a vigorous attack was made upon the required study of the Greek language as a condition of an academic degree. The attack was made presumably on the ground that the results of the study when viewed in a practical light appeared small and unsatisfactory—too small for the time devoted to it. If, indeed, the attack had been made, not upon the study of the language, but upon the *method* by which the language has been taught and studied in our schools, it would have been a just attack and might have resulted in greater good. But there is something better than the visible and tangible, the outward and the perishable. And the Greek language, with the immortal literature which it enshrines, has been prized and cherished most for its power to discipline the mind, to purify the intellectual vision, to liberate, refine, enrich, and ennoble the inward man, the immortal man. But in order that this discipline, refinement, culture, mental wealth may be attained in the highest degree, the language must be acquired as a living language and made a part of the individual being so that it shall be a perennial source of life and strength and shall make the man once more a man forever.

Born as we are, heirs to but a single tongue, on this side of the Atlantic, when we acquire a foreign tongue—the Greek, for instance—as it is acquired in our schools, the first degree of the mastery of the language consists in the ability to translate it by means of a grammar and lexicon into the English. Another degree of mastery consists in the ability to translate the English by means of a grammar and lexicon into the Greek. A higher degree of mastery, which is not attained because it is not sought, consists in the ability to take the language in through the ear, to understand it when we hear it spoken. The highest degree of mastery consists in the power to think in it and feel in it, and to speak it with ease and without friction.

And the degree of the discipline which a study imparts is in the direct ratio of the degree of the mastery of that study.

The highest mastery, therefore, is the highest discipline. If, then, we would attain the highest discipline which the Greek language with its wealth of literature may be made to yield, we must acquire it as a living language by living methods. And if we would be practical and would acquire it as a modern tongue for practical purposes, we must yet acquire it as a living language by living methods. And the first step in the direction of such an acquisition is to put ourselves in relations with it as a living language, to accept it as a living language, meant first for the ear, not for the eye; to pronounce it as the living Greeks themselves to-day pronounce it, and to converse in it until the ear becomes accustomed to it and the mind through the ear takes hold of it and makes it a possession forever.

And reasons why we should pronounce it as it is pronounced in the land where it has ever lived and still lives in the freshness and beauty of immortal youth are given by the learned and enthusiastic Dr. Rose, to whom all friends and lovers of Greek owe a debt of genuine and lasting gratitude.

REMARKS BY HON. D. N. BOTASSI, CONSUL GENERAL OF GREECE.

After the admirable and exhaustive paper which my learned friend, Dr. Rose, read before you, it would be a presumption on my part to try and add anything, at least to the literary side, so I will limit myself to a few general remarks.

When Erasmus published his famous treatise in 1528, Greece was simply a geographical denomination, a Turkish province in fact, having been conquered by the Turks ten years after the fall of Constantinople, which, as you know, occurred in the year 1453. Few people then paid any attention how Greek was pronounced in that Turkish province called Greece, which had changed masters so many times, having been under the Romans, Franks, Venetians, and the Turks.

Greek was considered then a dead language, like the Latin and Hebrew, and the savants from that time on adopted unhesitatingly the Erasmian pronunciation as the correct one.

But the Greek Revolution of 1821, which ended in the establishment of the present Greek kingdom in 1830, put a new aspect on the existing state of things. It was almost a revelation! Old Hellas rose from her ashes like the phœnix of mythology, with Athens for her capital, with her cities called Piræus, Sparta, Corinth, and Pylos, as of old, with her Marathon and Salamis, with her Acropolis and its immortal Parthenon.

The Greek language was preserved from generation to generation in that extreme corner of Southern Europe chiefly through the Greek church. The Turks, fortunately for the Greeks, left public worship free, and the reading of the New Testament and the liturgies of St. Basil and of St. John Chrysostom were heard every

Sunday from one end of Greece to the other in their original purity.

With the establishment of schools and colleges the people's vernacular was gradually purified from the intermixture of foreign words, and now the language of the Athenian newspapers and of the government despatches differs very little from the language of the New Testament, which is, as you know, ancient Greek in a simplified form, commonly called the Alexandrine Greek.

This is a wonderful achievement in sixty-five years, which is the length of the political life of Greece. Modern Greek is nothing else but ancient Greek in a modified form. The orthography, accents, aspirants, etc., are absolutely like the old Greek. It is now a complete language for the conveyance of human thought, and we have at present many prose writers and poets who have acquired a European reputation. You would be astonished to hear how pleasantly it sounds to one's ears, to hear the song of Hiawatha translated into modern Greek, as well as some of the plays of Shakespeare, like "King Lear," "Romeo and Juliet," and "Hamlet."

Modern Greek is now spoken by ten millions of people, for, besides the present Greek kingdom, numbering over two and a half millions, Greek is extensively spoken in European Turkey, Bulgaria, Servia, Roumania, Southern Russia, through all the northern coast of the Black Sea, and thence from Trebizonde and Sinope to Constantinople and down to the coast of Asia Minor, the ancient Ionia, from Smyrna down to Beyrout and Alexandria. One can travel through all those countries to-day and get along very well if he knows no other language than modern Greek. It is absurd, therefore, to call a language spoken by over ten millions of Greeks a dead language, and it is a matter of deep regret that, owing to the prevailing Erasmian pronunciation in your colleges, your young men cannot ask for a glass of water and be understood in Athens, although they spent many years of their life in learning Greek in America.

I will not detain you any longer. Dr. Rose brought the strongest argument to prove why the modern Greek pronunciation should be universally adopted in America. I will finish my remarks with a recitation of a few verses from the heroic poem of one of our celebrated modern poets, Alexander Soutzo, called ὁ Περιπλανώμενος, viz.: "The Wanderer."

Χώρα μεγαλοφυίας; εἰς τοὺς κόλπους σου τὸ πάλαι
'Ω πατρίς μου, αἱ ἰδέαι ἀνεβλάστανον μεγάλαι,
Καὶ τυραννοκτόνον ξίφος κρύπτοντες εἰς τὰς μυρσίνας
Οἱ 'Αρμόδιοι ἀνώρθουν ἰσονόμους τὰς 'Αθήνας.
῎Αλλοτε θεοὶ ἐπάτουν τὰ ἐδάφη σου καὶ θείαν
῞Εως σήμερον ἡ γῆ σου ἀναδίδει εὐωδίαν
 Καὶ ἡ αὔρα τοῦ Ζεφύρου
Ψιθυρίζει τὴν ἀρχαίαν μελωδίαν τοῦ 'Ομήρου.

Δύω ἔφερε μοχθοῦσα Γίγαντας τῆς γῆς ἡ σφαῖρα,
Καὶ τῶν δύω οἱ αἰῶνες σὲ κηρύττουσι μητέρα.
Στρατηλάτης τῶν 'Ελλήνων ἐκδικῶν τὸν Μαραθῶνα
Ο 'Αλέξανδρος εἰσῆλθε νικητὴς εἰς Βαβυλῶνα.
Διετήρει αἵματός σου εἰς τὰς φλέβας του ρανίδα,
'Ο Κορσικανὸς ὁ ἔχων τὸ Ταύγετον πατρίδα
 Καὶ εἰς μίαν μόνην ὥραν
Τὴν γῆν παίξας, τὴν γῆν χάσας εἰς τοῦ Βατερλῶ τὴν χώραν.

'Αλλ' ὁ πρῶτος ἀγαπῶν σε καὶ τὴν δόξαν τῶν 'Ελλήνων
Πέραν τοῦ 'Ινδοῦ καὶ Γάγγου μέχρι Τροπικοῦ ἐκτείνων,
'Απεβίωσε μονάρχης καὶ ὡς τοῦ πολέμου λείαν
Μίαν ἔδωκεν εἰς πάντα στρατηγὸν του βασιλείαν.
'Ο δὲ δεύτερος μισῶν σε καὶ τὸν ἄδοξον Σουλτάνον
'Επιστήθιόν του φίλον ἀντὶ σοῦ παραλαμβάνων
 Δέσμιος εἰς νῆσον ξένην,
Δέσμιος εἰς τὴν 'Αγίαν ἐτελεύτησεν 'Ελένην. . . .

William J. Seelye, Professor of Greek, Wooster University, Ohio, lectured on the same subject, the Pronunciation of Greek, almost simultaneously with me. I saw his excellent scholarly paper, which is published in the transactions of College Association of Ohio for 1896, only when my book was partly in type.

CHAPTER III.

THE BYZANTINES.*

THE Byzantine Empire, otherwise called the East Roman, the Romaic, the Oriental, the Greek Empire, was created when Theodosius the Great, before his death in 395, divided the Roman Empire between his two sons.

In the first days of September, 476, the Occidental empire of the Romans ceased to be.

When the Roman Empire was dying out, it had the good fortune to be absorbed in the life of Greece, and it derived from that union a renewed energy which secured for it another millennium of existence.

The absorption of the Roman into the Byzantine Empire was a blessing to civilization and to mankind.

The conquests of Philip and Alexander the Great had had the effect of widely extending Hellenism throughout the East. This extension

* Lecture delivered before the Society for Literary Knowledge, New York, in March, 1897.

received a new impulse from the unity of the government of the new—that is, the Byzantine—Roman Empire over the whole civilized world. Then came Christianity, which borrowed from Hellenism its language, and also contributed to spread the influence of Greek letters and Greek culture beyond the limits which geography would have assigned. In the end the Greek language was spoken as far as the Danube on the north and Armenia and the Euphratus on the east; and all these Greek-speaking countries gradually united into a sort of a mixed world, which constituted the Byzantine Empire.

Until recently the Byzantine era was the least known and the most obscure in the field of historical study. When the Greeks, by a heroic struggle lasting seven years (from 1821 to 1828), had regained their independence from Turkish bondage they received the full and enthusiastic sympathy of the civilized world.

Nevertheless, the history of the Byzantines, of their Greek and Christian state of over a thousand years of existence, was still treated with great injustice, exaggerated severity, and contempt.

To the popular imagination the Byzantine

Empire appeared as a political monstrosity in which one incapable emperor succeeded another, each putting out the eyes of his predecessor, an empire in which romantic scenes of bloodshed, barbarous cruelty, and stormy disputes over dogmatic questions were the rule.

The hatred toward the Greeks, who, as the outpost of Christendom, have been fighting the battle of civilization against the world of barbarism, and havé succumbed only after a heroic resistance of a thousand years, has its source in religious dissensions, and has been taken up by ignoramuses who took no interest even in questions of religion.

The empire of the East fell four hundred years ago and was thereby silenced. The West survived, and until recently has had the talk all its own way. It has used the opportunity in the full spirit of the rancor which already animated it. There is an abundant anti-Hellenic literature by a numerous body of writers who during many years have undertaken to enlighten the European public.

National intercourse, which is characteristic of our time, will gradually efface the traditions begotten in ignorance. The impartial decisions of the latest learned and critical Western writers have already brought a great deal of light and justice.

During the last decade no part of history has received more attention than the Byzantine period. Krumbacher's *Byzantinische Zeitschrift*, a periodical devoted to the study of Byzantine history, language, literature, and art, has reached its sixth year. The six volumes contain contributions from the pens of the best scholars, philologists, archæologists, historians of all the civilized countries, articles and communications in German, English, French, Italian, and Greek. The scholars of the different countries co-operate assiduously to enlighten us, to do justice where there had been a tendency to do injustice.

Six years ago Krumbacher, A. Ehrhard, and H. Gelzer published an elaborate work on the history of the Byzantine literature. The appearance of a second edition more than twice as large as the first gives evidence that researches in this direction are appreciated. The attention of the world of learning is again directed to the Byzantines in order to vindicate the truth and render tardy justice where for four centuries both had been denied.

When we compare the history of the Roman Empire of the East with the Roman Empire of the German nation, each with a history of a thousand years; when we see what influence the Empire of the East had on the Empire of the West, and which influence culminated at the period of the Renaissance, we will no longer treat the history of the Byzantines with contempt.

The history of the Byzantines is one of unceasing and unwearied activity. Christian Constantinople, from the hour of her foundation to that in which her sun finally set in blood, was engaged in constant struggles against successive hordes of barbarians and foreign adventurers.

The facts that the old monarchy of Constantine and of Theodosius, although much divided and diminished, resisted the repeated attacks of masses of Persians, Bulgarians, Slavs, Arabians, Turks; that it rose after every deep humiliation; that it withstood the severest catastrophe—namely, the destruction of the empire by the knights of the fourth crusade, the loss of the capital at the Golden Horn, before it sank under the Osmans—these remarkable facts should incite us to familiarize ourselves with the *true* history of an empire of such wonderful, of such exceptional vitality.

During several centuries the Byzantine Empire could more than once be compared to an immense fortress simultaneously attacked and besieged from all sides. Her vast borders—extending from the Apennines to Jerusalem, from the Syrtes to the mountainous regions of Armenia—had to be repeatedly defended against the enemies of half the world.

Within, she had to fight heresy after heresy, but succeeded nevertheless in raising the edifice of the Church upon solid and enduring foundations, and at the same time, by preserving and completing the Roman legislation, she established principles of jurisprudence which are recognized to-day throughout the civilized world.

We have to lay great stress on the most extraordinary significance of the Byzantine Empire: from the end of the Roman reign, the Byzantines were the heirs and preservers of a highly developed civilization and of the treasures of antique culture. It is true that the Byzantine literature could not rival the productions of earlier ages, but it preserved none the less the traditions of the intellectual splendor of Greece.

The time when the Turkish cannon made an opening into the gigantic walls of Constantinople corresponds to the period when the Western countries—thanks to the Byzantines, now strong and happy—developed the new culture and gave asylum to the last representatives of Greek learning.

There are three writers especially who have done a great deal to promulgate error and injustice in regard to Byzantine history, namely, Montesquieu, Gibbon, and, to a limited extent, Fallmerayer. Since, however, historians like Zinkeisen, Finlay, Ross, Curtius, Hopf, and Mendelssohn-Bartholdi have made scientific researches, there are few, and there should be none, who will form a judgment upon the Byzantines, based upon no other, no better, no later source than the three first-named writers upon the history of mediæval Greece. Still every day we meet people who have by tradition, without personal research into the facts, accepted the most absurd ideas about the Byzantines. It is on account of such people that it may appear proper to consider the writings of the two first-named historians, Montesquieu and Gibbon, and later on to speak of Fallmerayer.

Montesquieu treats of the Roman period in a masterly manner; the subject of the Byzantine epoch, however, is beyond his depth; here he is superficial and prejudiced. He informs us in a general way that from the period of Phokas onward the history of the Greek Empire is a mere tissue of rebellion, conspiracy, and treachery. He says: "The emperors were led by the nose by the monks and priests, who became all powerful after their triumph over the iconoclasts. . . . If any one will compare the Greek clergy with the Latin clergy, and the conduct of the Popes with that of the Patriarchs of Constantinople, he will see on the one side men as wise as those on the other side were silly." These quotations are in themselves quite enough. As for the reasons by which Montesquieu proposes to explain the fact that the Byzantine Empire lasted for more than a millennium, they are simply self-contradictory.

The history of an empire which endured for a thousand years cannot be given by being crumpled up into a few contemptuous sentences, as Montesquieu has done, especially not when that history presents complications probably greater than those of any other empire.

"The truth is," says Bikelas (of whose lectures on Christian Greece, delivered at the Cercle St. Simon in Paris in the year 1885, I avail myself to some extent for this paper), "that it has been only by enveloping the shallowness of his historical judgments upon Christian and imperial Constantinople in the glittering phantasmagoria of a witty style and an audacious dogmatism that Montesquieu has succeeded so largely in inducing posterity to swallow his aphorisms."

Gibbon has given the history of the Byzantines in a monumental work, written in an entirely partial manner; he has allowed his judgment to be biassed by his prejudices, and has written with the express aim and object of propounding and supporting his own preconceived ideas. The fundamental principle of his theory is that Christianity was the cause alike of the ruin of ancient civilization, of the decline and fall of the Roman Empire, and of all the misery and darkness of the Middle Ages.

Almost on every page, at least on every occasion, he shows his hatred toward the Greeks, which goes so far that it is his custom to qualify the word "Greek" by some depreciatory adjective. Altogether Gibbon has written history as it should not be and as it is not, as a rule, written any more. However, Gibbon's theory of history is but one instance of a feature which is only too characteristic of the English mind. Many an act of the English people toward the Greeks can be explained by the same trait.

"The Byzantine Empire," says Bikelas, "was predestined to perform in particular one great work in human history: that work was to preserve civilization during the period of barbarism which we call the Middle Ages. For the performance of that work no abundant originality was needful. The mission of Christian Constantinople was not to create, but to save; and that mission she fulfilled for the benefit of the Europe of the future. It is not just on the part of the modern world, which has thus profited thereby, to refuse to its benefactors the tribute of this gratitude, and still less so when it caricatures history in order to lessen the apparent burden of its indebtedness."

The first fundamental principle is that the Byzantine Empire was built on the most perfect centralization. This principle of the Byzantines found its best support in the site, and thereby in the military and commercial significance of the capital, of Constantinople. The history of nine centuries from Justinian I. to the entrance of Mahomet II. into the blood-soaked streets of Byzantium shows what great ideas Constantine had in view when he founded his new residence. Since the day on which he transferred the seat of government to the Bosphorus it has from century to century become more apparent what wonderful offensive and defensive strength the new capital could develop against attacks, and what great advantages its site offered in keeping together a reign extending into three continents. Constantinople during the time of the Byzantines until the days of terror of the Frankish conquest in 1204 was a marvellously beautiful city and at the same time the most powerful military stronghold of the whole Middle Ages.

Against the attacks of all the hordes which the Byzantines had to fight before the year 1204 the city was almost invulnerable, especially since they had in the Greek sea fire a weapon of most terrific effect. This fire was the invention of a Greek, Kallinikos of Heliopolis. It consisted of a mixture of combustibles, containing naphtha, sulphur, pitch, and other ingredients, which burned even under water. When the incendiary ships with their copper cylinders containing the composition for the destructive fire came near to the battle-ships of the enemy the latter was overtaken by fright and fear. The formula of the composition was kept a state secret. The Byzantines were enabled repeatedly to destroy large masses of enemies under the walls of their capital, and thus to save an empire which otherwise would have been lost.

The imperial government has been accused

of neglecting material interests. It is not history alone, however, that tells of the supremacy of the Greek world throughout the whole of the Middle Ages in matters which insure the well-being of a state, but the ruins of public works, ruins which savagery has left, show us that the subjects of this empire had no ground for casting on their rulers the reproaches which Western European writers so persistently repeat.

The history of nations, as that of states, as a rule represents epochs of decadence and of greatness, and thus it is with the Byzantines.

For us Americans it is especially interesting to study the history of a state which, like our own republic, was not built upon a national basis. The empire presented since Justinian a multiform mixture of different Latin and Greek colonists alongside a strong body of real Greeks; in addition to these came the descendants of the old Egyptians, and quite imposing numbers of Semites and Berbers.

Empress Irene, an Athenian, excepted, we find, until the end of the Basilides—*i.e.*, until the middle of the eleventh century—Latin, Asiatic, and Græco-Slavic emperors wielding the sceptre at the Golden Horn. Only the last dynasties of the Komnenes, of the Dukas, of the Angelos, of the Palæologi were real Greeks.

It was not until after the decline of the Byzantine Empire that the Byzantines began to call themselves Hellenes and their monarchy emperors of the Hellenes. Up to that time the autocrats were called Augusti and the subjects Romans. This custom has proved so deep-rooted that it not only still survives as the universal usage of the East, but even in such writers as Byron we find the Hellenic language termed "Romaic." At the same time the inhabitants of Hellas proper were not called Hellenes but Helladikoi, and the ancient and glorious word Hellene was employed (by usage possibly imitated from the New Testament) in a deprecatory sense, to indicate an idolater.

Constantinople had been founded not as a Greek, but as a Latin city. From the beginning, however, Greeks were in considerable numbers among the inhabitants. Greek cities and provinces had been forced to give a great many of their magnificent works of art to ornament the new capital. In the development of the empire the whole population assumed a more and more Greek character. Exactly as it is to-day, the beautiful city on the Bosphorus with its gay life, a place where wealth could be gained, became attractive to many Greeks from the islands, from Asia Minor, from Macedonia, from Thessaly, Epirus, and Achaia. This regular immigration increased during the first two centuries of its existence while northern barbarians invaded Greece and devastated the country and smaller cities.

History shows that, in relative opposition of the Græcized peoples to the Greeks of the old Greek colonies, and all Greeks in the ethnographic sense of the word, the genuine Greeks have always maintained a predominating position: first, on account of their influence on the ethnographic and linguistic composition of the mixed Hellenism in the population of the capital; secondly, on account of the strength peculiar to their nation (this strength having by no means been lost, nor has it been to this very day); and, finally, on account of their excellent influence in politics, most marked and significant during the time of the Komnenes. Through these a new phase of the empire was developed.

Those who, when Constantinople fell, fled from the ruin, bearing with them the treasures of the wisdom of their ancient forefathers, well deserved the name of Hellenes, which they assumed.

The emperors reigned under conditions which had developed in the political new-formation or creation of Constantine the Great. They represented in their person the majesty, the unity, and the coherence of the empire. The emperor had control of the army and navy, of the external politics, of the executives, and of an essential part of the legislative power. All this constituted on the one hand the strength of the autocracy and explains on the other hand its temporary weakness. The fundamental construction, the essential institutions were so well founded that this remarkable organization, the Byzantine Empire, maintained itself while weak and even decidedly bad emperors governed. It endured repeatedly, without actually endangering its existence, during the severest crises. It required the work of a century of the miserable dynasty of the Angelos to enable Enrico Dandolos and the Knighthood of Lombardy, Burgundy, Champagne, and Flanders to gain the victory over the Byzantines, in the year 1204.

The condition of the vast empire during the six or seven centuries from Justinian I. until the fourth crusade was only very exceptionally such that the position of a Byzantine emperor would have been considered enviable, or as the highest degree of earthly happiness. The situation continually demanded men of a high sense of duty and understanding of their enormous task, men of great talents and excellent training for their vocation, men of great vigor and perseverance. By no means was the throne always occupied by men who excelled in the princely attributes mentioned, still less were they always men of such type as the circumstances, sometimes very difficult, would have required.

During more than a millennium, from the accession of Arcadius in 395 to the heroic death of Constantine XIII. in 1453, the Eastern Empire was governed by a succession of eighty-one emperors. Of these eighty-one autocrats seventy-three can be assigned to one or other of the ten dynasties. Each of these dynasties comprises a group of persons who succeeded one another upon the throne either by right of blood, or by reason of the imperial will and the consent of the regnant family, of which they were the representatives and, in one sense, the members and perpetuators. The continuity of the ten Byzantine dynasties was broken only by seven isolated princes, the duration of whose combined reigns amounts to about thirty years.

With these facts before us we find it difficult to understand the historians who write: Momentous was often the circumstance that there existed no regular order of succession to the throne. Imposing or meritorious emperors, who enjoyed great popularity, were well able to testate the crown to their sons or even their widows, and thus we find a whole number of dynasties. It is true, however, that when in the nature of things a change of rulers was in view, bloody palace revolts, cowardly murder, and open acts of atrocity occurred during the long history of the Byzantine Empire as well as during the history of other empires. The influence of women of the court, of powerful ministers, but also of eunuchs which came more and more into the foreground became significant in such moments. We shall see later on how much all this was due to the unavoidable influence of barbarism.

Of the seventy-six emperors and five empresses who occupied the Byzantine throne fifteen were put to death, seven were blinded or otherwise mutilated, four were deposed and imprisoned in monasteries, and ten were compelled to abdicate. "This list," says Bikela, from whose book I have copied it, "comprising nearly half of the whole number, is a sufficient indication of the horrors by which the history of the empire is only too often marked, and it may be frankly admitted that these dark stains, disfiguring pages which but for them would be bright with the things that were beautiful and glorious, go some way to excuse if not justify the obloquy which Western writers have been so prone to cast upon the East. But it is not by considering the evil only, any more than the good only, that it is possible to form a correct opinion of an historical epoch. To judge the Byzantine Empire only by the crimes which defiled the palace would be as unjust as if the French people were to be estimated by nothing but the massacre of St. Bartholomew, the Reign of Terror, and the Commune of 1871."

Notwithstanding the existence of the Christian Church in the Byzantine Empire, the continual and uninterrupted contact of the Byzantines with the barbaric elements by which they were surrounded from the beginning to the end of their existence explains the lamented incidents in their history. The Byzantine people, although in every respect the superiors of their contemporaries, could not altogether escape from the influence of their neighbors; they, however, were the guardians of classical civilization and were Christians, and strove to keep above the deluge of barbarism by which the rest of the world was then inundated. When modern writers accuse the Byzantines of cruelty they seem to forget that their contemporaries in Western Europe had manners and principles of jurisprudence which were marked by a ferocity unapproached by anything in Byzantine despotism. Bikela refers to executions of Dolino in Italy and of Hugh the Defender (the young) in England, to the murderers of James I. in Scotland, and to the whole history of the processes against the templars or the lepers in France; to the peculiar sentence of high treason in England, often fully carried out within the last century, and even pronounced in Ireland in the present century; to the legislation of England with regard to religion, and especially its application during the sixteenth century; to the execution of the last Inca of Peru by the Spanish Government, and of Damiens by the French. Bikelas, however, does not mention the Spanish Inquisition, the chambers of torture, especially in Germany, the *institutio criminalis Carolina*, the tortures to which supposed witches were subjected even in our own country.

The most deplorable epoch in the history of the Byzantine Empire, the period in which assassination and mutilation most abounded, was that in which it was exposed to the influence of the crusaders and thus brought in contact with Western Europe. During the twenty years between 1183 to 1204, six emperors occupied the shaky throne of the East; all of them were deposed, two of them were blinded, and all were put to death, except Isaac II., who anticipated the executioner by dying in prison.

No nation can boast of an immaculate history. The French kingdom, the unity of the Catholic Church of the Middle Ages, and Protestantism have been established through all sorts of crimes and errors. A great man even is constituted by his faults as much as by his good qualities. The roughness, the harsh ways of Napoleon formed to some extent his strength. Had he been well trained, polite, modest, he would not have succeeded; he would have been no more powerful than we are.

If we are to judge the Byzantine court by its fruits, we shall see that it was not, as some writers maintain, the abode of frivolity and effeminacy. It is true for a time a herd of eunuchs dishonored the imperial palaces, and altogether many crimes were committed within their walls; on the other hand, however, manly virtue was never long lacking to the Byzantine throne, and the majority of the sovereigns who occupied it showed themselves worthy of their exalted station. This can be proved by the following extract from history:

In the sixth century Justinian I. reigned for over forty years. As a conqueror he restored to the Roman army its ancient fame; as a sovereign he adorned with great buildings not only his capital, but cities located in his remotest provinces; as a legislator he took a place in the history of jurisprudence which has made his name immortal.

The seventh century is filled by the great name of Heraclius, who, in his victorious wars against the Persians, resumed and continued the work of Alexander the Great. His great-grandson, Constantine IV., was faithful to the glorious traditions of his progenitor, and by his brave resistance to the repeated expeditions of the Arabs against Constantinople stemmed the tide of Mohammedan conquest and earned the title of Deliverer of Europe.

In the eighth century Leo III., the savior of Constantinople and reformer of the empire, gave a new impulse to the Byzantine world.

In the ninth century Basil I. crowned the work of Justinian I. by his final codification of Roman law, and exalted the power of the empire, which under him and his successors enjoyed a lengthened period of greatness and prosperity.

In the tenth century Nikophorus II., John I., and Basil II. (the Bulgar slayer) fought gloriously against the Mohammedans and the Bulgars.

In the twelfth century three successive monarchs of the house of the Komnenes, Alexis I., his son John II., and his grandson, the heroic Manuel I., in the midst of every variety of plot and distraction, saved the dignity of the throne and preserved the safety of the state.

In the thirteenth century Theodore I. and John III. rallied the national forces in the midst of calamities and shed lustre upon the imperial crown, till the day when Michael VIII., by the reconquest of Constantinople, opened the way to a new period in the history of the Eastern Empire. And these are not the only Byzantine emperors whose names shine gloriously in history. Ignorance and spite have for a long time combined to cast obscurity over the renown of some, but the impartiality of more modern writers is at length beginning to do justice to their memory.

It is not to the throne alone that we must look in order to find the great names of Byzantine history. Through the whole course of the empire's existence, there were never lacking eminent men who preserved the best traditions of the classical ages. In every period there arose illustrious soldiers, able statesmen, good and saintly ecclesiastics, and men of learning to whom the Greek nation owes at least the almost unique advantage of possessing, in its own language, its own annals for an unbroken period of more than twenty centuries.

From the very foundation of Constantinople, with the afflux of more and more Greeks to this new capital, a most important factor was at work to complete its character, namely, the influence of the Christian Church.

The conversion of Constantine the Great and his house to the new world religion promoted the Christian cause to a high degree. The development of the Greek nation under the influence of Christianity is highly interesting. The world language of the East, the elegant language of conversation and literature of the new Roman Empire between the Adria and the Euphratus had become the language of the Church, and this circumstance contributed largely in giving the new capital, Constantinople, a Greek physiognomy. The Christian religion took root on Greek soil. It was embraced not only by the poor and humbler classes, but also by the educated Greeks with their acute intellect, inclined especially to dialectic activity regarding the dogmatics of the new religion. They had inherited philosophic speculation and dialectic cunning from the antique Greek philosophers, and this inheritance which they now applied to theological questions became subsequently dangerous to them since it led to religious dissensions.

Montreuil says: "The Greeks are by their very nature philosophical and speculative. The search for abstract truth is to them more attractive than the pursuit of reforms or the regulation of manners. They are a race eminently literary. They have always been thinkers rather than statesmen. They accordingly seized upon that side of theology which appealed most strongly to their natural genius. The heresies which arose among them were begotten by the same spirit which is manifest through the whole history of their race.

"The unity of the Church was saved by the councils. These assemblies dealt with the heresies and eradicated them; they defined the doctrines and ratified the organization of the Church. The territory of the Byzantine Empire was the locality where the councils met. Their conduct was animated from first to last by the keenness of the Greek intellect, which, now clothed in its Byzantine phase, here offered to the service of the Gospel the same natural gifts which had once produced all that was best in thought of the old Hellenic world."

The Greek inclination to partisanship showed itself in regard to religious matters to an extraordinary degree. The fiercest fights between orthodoxy and heterodoxy inflamed the Greeks for centuries, lasting far into the Middle Ages, and often disturbed the public peace; but eventually they all ceased, never to return. In firm tenacity the Greeks adhere to the orthodox, the Anatolic Church, and their religion has become as well marked a part of their nationality as the religion of Homer and Plato was characteristic of the old Hellas.

It must be confessed that unceasing disputes,

now about a word, and again about a syllable, have not added to the glory of the empire. There were times when Constantinople was converted into a vast theological seminary, in which everybody took part in controversies. "If you ask a person," says Gregorius of Nyssa, "about coins, he delivers a discourse about γεννητὸν and ἀγέννητον. You inquire concerning the price of bread; the baker informs you that the son is subordinate to the father. If you wish to know whether the bath is in good order, the answer is: 'The son was created out of nothing.'"

Perhaps the controversies were so lively at Constantinople because the intelligent and cultivated people found in them a field for the exercise of their mental activity, which was not furnished them by printed matter, by newspapers or telegrams, or by presidential elections. With the Byzantines religion was an object of public interest. The fact, however, that there was a war in Germany between Protestants and Catholics, lasting thirty years, and the records of the Spanish Inquisition, show how questions of conscience have excited human passion in other countries likewise.

The question of truth in religion touched the Byzantine state more deeply than it did most states. They had to make the Church strong. The Church was the very foundation upon which rested the prosperity and even the preservation of the state. "The Greeks," says Montreuil, "felt toward their religion an attachment which amounted to fanaticism; their religious beliefs were the centre around which all other ideas were grouped; and the bond of religion was more powerful than any other in inspiring the Hellenic nationality with a lively, enduring unity."

The main feature which checked the power of the emperors was the Anatolic Church. Public opinion was controlled by the Church, and with this even emperors had to reckon. It is true that the Church was not able to suppress vice and passion to such an extent as to prevent the horrible manifestations of savagery, the cruelty of judicial proceedings, which often formed a direct contradiction to the otherwise brilliant civilization of the Byzantines; but Christian morality and Christian views had developed far enough, at least, to prevent entirely or temporarily such outrageous conduct as had been shown by not a few of the Roman emperors.

It is easy to understand why the intellectual life of the capital and also that of the provincial centres became more and more decidedly absorbed in ecclesiastical questions and interests. All higher interests for centuries were concentrated in ecclesiastical affairs. The powerful dogmatic fights which shook the empire like earthquakes, the long-continued wrestling of the parties in the image question, and still later the dogmatic war with Rome were by no means considered as a decided evil. The genius of the Byzantines found pleasure in these movements to such an extent that the repeated dogmatic parliamentary battles before the greater or lesser synods appeared to them almost of more importance than the actual fights of the legions with the barbaric peoples at the Danube, the Balkans, and Strymon, and with the overwhelming masses of Islam.

It has been admitted in the foregoing remarks that the population sometimes devoted an excessive amount of attention to theological discussions, and it must be further conceded that there were periods when the development of monasticism was anything but beneficial to the state, when monasteries were universal to excess, when the clergy became a danger to the state, and finally contributed to the fall of Constantinople. On the other hand, historic truth compels us to accord the monastic orders the just praise which is their due for spreading Christianity and Christian civilization among the barbarous nations, since while they preached the Gospel they taught letters and art. The Slavonic language was reduced to writing by the two Greek monks Cyril and Methodius, and Greek monks were the teachers of Ulphilas, the principal apostle and civilizer of the Goths. .

"The free Greece of to-day, moreover," says Bikelas, "can never forget her everlasting debt to the monasteries of her church, which were centres of national life and national culture, as well as of national religion during the ages of her bondage."

On the whole, the administration of the finances of the Byzantines was economical. Excellent statesmen and financiers succeeded, during the good times of the empire, in accumulating larger sums in the treasury than any other power during the earlier part of the Middle Ages. Nothwithstanding this, there were periods of senseless extravagance and unscrupulous corruption. But even in this direction a bad government could not go too far, because of the development of principles which nobody could overstep without danger to himself. For instance, it was considered absolutely unpardonable to reduce the value of the normal gold coin of the empire. Those emperors who were successful in reducing the taxes were sure of the greatest popularity. Extortions, when not justified by extremely dangerous conditions of the state, were revenged by bloody revolts, sometimes of a cruel character. The readiness and the fighting power of the army corresponded exactly with the flourishing and well-regulated state of the finances.

To Finlay belongs the eminent and scholarly credit of having contradicted and completely dispelled the general belief in the military feebleness and incompetency of the Byzantines.

The Byzantine soldiery was recruited from among the most warlike races of both the Greek and the barbarian population of the Empire. They were in tactics and arms superior to every enemy against whom they had to contend. They were often braver than they got the credit of having been. They knew how to fight when they could not count on victory. The continued invasions constantly brought against them hordes of new enemies with new modes of warfare and new terrors. But Byzantine soldiers never refused the challenge. Under Heraclius and John Tzimiskis they glowed with enthusiasm; under Leo VI. they knew how to face their fate and do their duty. It is true the Greeks were first overcome by the Latins, but finally they were victorious over them. As already mentioned, long-continued bad government gave the Frankish adventurers the advantage. The wealth of the provinces contributed largely to the treasury; the sums which would have served to render armies efficient and provinces happy were squandered by the emperors at that period to furnish amusements for the inhabitants of the capital or to feed the luxurious splendor of the imperial court.

By looking at the incessant succession of enemies who never left the Byzantine government a moment of respite from attack, we shall be able to form a fair idea as to what must have been the strength and vitality of the empire itself, and what the extent of the service it rendered to Europe, to the cause of civilized humanity.

The first adversary against whom the Byzantines had to contend were the Goths. About eighty years before the foundation of Constantinople these savages crossed the Dniester and the Danube and devastated the country far and wide. Constantine brought them into subjection. They rebelled again under Theodosius the Great and were, after a long struggle, subdued anew. After Theodosius' death they commenced their invasion under Alaric. At length they were checked by the imperial armies, and the East was delivered from this plague and danger to civilization. "If they had taken root," says Bikela, "and founded states in the East, as they did in Italy, Gaul, and Spain; if the Byzantine world had been engulfed beneath the flood of their immigration, the history of the human race would have been a different one from that which it has been. If the East had been barbarized by the Goths as was the West, and the Eastern Empire had been destroyed, from what material would the European Renaissance have sprung?"

About a century and a half after Alaric, Belisarius and Narses, the generals of Justinian, crushed the Gothic power in Italy, and destroyed the Vandals in Africa. These military victories aided the regeneration of social life and order in these countries.

After the Byzantines had rendered such great service to Italy by fighting the Goths and had helped to preserve culture in the West, it is one of the most regrettable parts of Byzantine history that their excessive interference in affairs purely Italian brought on the rupture between the Eastern and the Western churches.

After the Goths came the Huns. These hordes, gradually advancing from Asia into Europe, made their appearance in the fifth century under Attila. He ravaged Thrace and Macedonia and imposed a humiliating peace upon the government of Constantinople, which happened to be represented at the time by a child and a woman, namely, Theodosius II. and his sister, the Empress Pulcheria. When, however, in course of time the husband of the latter, the Emperor Marcia, ascended the throne, and Attila sent to demand the continuance of the tribute, he was met with the reply: "I have iron for Attila, but no gold!" Attila moved away westward, spreading devastation and terror around him, till the day when Ætius broke the power of the Huns upon the plain of Chalons-sur-Marne.

In the sixth century the Avans poured down from the region of the Volga. In the time of Justinian II. and that of his successor, they devastated Byzantine provinces. Priscus, the general of the Emperor Maurice, at last subdued them in the year 600. But twenty years later they advanced, in alliance with the Persians, to the very walls of Constantinople and plundered the suburbs. The siege itself was in vain, the Avans retired, and never afterward played an important part in the history of the empire. The deliverance of the capital from these barbarians is still commemorated by the Church in the use of the 'Ανάθιστος ῾Υμνος, which was composed to celebrate it.

The consequences of the incursions of the Slav tribes were much more permanent than those produced by any other barbarous nation. The first Slavs who attacked the empire, after having seized Dacia, were subdued by the Great Justinian. Nevertheless Slavs continued to move forward till they entered even Greece itself.

From this time onward, sometimes as allies, sometimes as enemies, sometimes as subjects, and sometimes as prisoners, the Slavs scattered themselves over the empire, and at last took permanent possession of the settlements in which they are still to be found. From the sixth to the eighth century Slav invasions of Greece were frequent, and it is upon this fact that Fallmerayer based his famous theory to the effect that the Hellenes are extinct and that Hellas is now peopled by a Slav population.

In the older works on the history of Greece before the time of the Osmans, the history of Athens from the year 529 to the time of Basilios II. is almost a blank.

In the year 1835 the celebrated Fallmerayer, at the time the best instructed man about New Greek matters, received some documents from the contents of which he tried to prove that Athens, about the time of Justinian I., had been overwhelmed by masses of the Slavic army and had been devastated; that the Athenians had then left the city and had retired to Salamis, where they had spent four hundred years in exile, during which time the monumental splendor of Athens had been destroyed and the city transformed into a wood of olive-trees; that in the year 746 these woods, together with what little had been left of the city, had been consumed by fire. This view has been held with a certain tenacity for some years in the world of learning. Researches made since, however, have furnished *conclusive evidence* of the spuriousness of the documents. Not only that, but historical facts have now been established to prove the uninterrupted existence of the city of Athens during the whole of the Middle Ages.

Napoleon, on December 26th, 1805, without

further preliminaries, pronounced and proclaimed through the *Moniteur:* "The dynasty of Naples has ceased to reign." Fallmerayer, perhaps admiring the style of the great man in deciding the fate of a nation, disposed of the Greeks in the following words: "The Hellenic race has died out in Europe." This bold assertion was made by him in the year 1830. For some years Fallmerayer gained an easy victory over numerous opponents who attacked him with much passion, but with insufficient philological and historical knowledge. Only one German scholar, the eminent Zinkeisen, has taken the proper course to contradict the ingenious annihilator of the Greeks. He disproved Fallmerayer's statements by means of a careful and systematic research of Byzantine historians, and thereby succeeded in exposing many errors and superficialities of that writer. After Zinkeisen came scientific men like Ludwig Ross, Ernst Curtius, and Carl Mendelssohn-Bartholdi, who aided in refuting Fallmerayer's theories completely.

This reiteration of Fallmerayer's error may appear superfluous, but it is not; for there are many people who have read Fallmerayer only and are ignorant of the fact that his statements have been refuted. The publications of this man of learning have produced some good results: they have caused one of the most obscure periods in the history of the Middle Ages to be thoroughly investigated by eminent scholars. These investigations have shown that the Greeks of to-day are the direct descendants of the ancient Greeks; and their war for independence from 1821 to 1828 is evidence that they are also the heirs of the immortal glory which lives in the annals of history of their ancestors.

Bikelas says in regard to the Fallmerayer theory: "Moreover, whether the Slavs overspread Greece or not, no one who has any knowledge of the actual phenomena could testify to anything but that their absorption has been complete. The entirely and exclusively Hellenic character of all the features, physical and intellectual, manifested by the present inhabitants of the country is a most striking fact, almost unique in history, a glorious mark of our race, and a wondrous proof of the intensity of our national vitality."

The Russians appear on the stage of history in the ninth century. Four times in two centuries did they set sail toward Constantinople, but their attempts failed.

In 956 Olga, a Russian princess, came to Constantinople, where she was baptized. By her Christianity was introduced into Russia. From that time the Russians were generally friendly to the empire.

The Bulgars, originally a Turkish tribe but who at present speak a Slavonic dialect, moved forward from the Volga to the Danube, invaded Thracia in 559 and menaced Constantinople. The city was saved by Belisarius. Thenceforth they were a source of continued trouble to the empire. The humanizing influence of Christianity seemed to have mitigated the savagery of the Bulgars, when toward the close of the tenth century a war broke out which was fiercer than ever. After a bloody struggle lasting thirty years Basil II., the Bulgar slayer, completely shattered their power in 1018, and Bulgaria was made a Byzantine province. One hundred and seventy years later they again rose in rebellion, after they had acknowledged the religious supremacy of the Pope. Nevertheless while the Latin dynasty was reigning in Constantinople, John, Kral of the Bulgarians, fought on the Greek side against the Franks.

The Magyars or Hungarians, another Turkish tribe, filled Europe with alarm until their power was destroyed by the German emperor Otto the Great.

In the end the empire succeeded, often by arms, at other times by diplomacy, but most of all by the influence of religion, commerce, and civilization, not only in protecting itself against the changes of these successive inroads, but in laying the foundation of civilization and even of future greatness amid these hostile barbarous tribes.

The Oriental enemies of the empire were of a different sort. In their case the Byzantine power had not to deal with barbarous tribes which might first be conquered, but could afterward be assimilated to the imperial state by the influences of civilization and Christianity. In the East, new Rome was called to wrestle with mighty nations possessed of a highly organized polity and animated by a special religious faith. Europe and Asia were thus brought face to face in implacable contrast and collision; the empire of the Byzantines is deserving of lasting gratitude for the long contention by which it continued the traditions of classical Hellas.

The continuity of these traditions was especially marked in the struggle of the empire with

Persia. The collision between these opposing forces was terrible. Whole armies perished; rich and fertile provinces were reduced to deserts. The deadly conflicts of so many centuries did not convince either Greeks or Persians of the futility of trying to alter the natural boundaries between the two empires. In the end the Persians were overcome by Heraclius, who after a long and glorious struggle imposed peace upon them in 628.

Since the days of Scipio and Hannibal no bolder enterprise has been attempted than that which Heraclius achieved for the deliverance of the empire. The peace he forced them to accept they never broke. From this time the Asiatic enemies of Christianity were no longer the Persians, but Mohammedans, first the Arabs, and afterward the Turks.

Jerusalem was captured by Omar in 637. The next year Egypt fell into the hands of Amron, after Alexandria had sustained a siege of fourteen months. Nine years later the Arabs conquered the remaining countries of Roman Africa, and in sixty more they destroyed the kingdom of the Goths and took possession of Spain. From Spain they passed into France, but the tide of their conquest, in that direction, was at length arrested forever by Charles Martel upon the plains of Tours in 732.

While Mohammedanism was thus pouring into Western Europe, Constantinople formed a barrier on the East which it utterly failed to surmount. Under Constantine IV. the Arabs assailed the dominions of the Byzantine Empire, and in 672 the imperial city itself sustained a siege of five months. The attempt was repeated in vain for seven consecutive years, and was followed in the end by a peace of thirty years' duration, but in 717 the Arabs again subjected the capital to a futile siege, which lasted thirteen months.

If they had succeeded in their first attempts, and conquered the European provinces of the Byzantine Empire, they would have been able to advance westward and unite their forces with those of their brethren who were moving northward out of Spain. In that event, we should have had no victory of Charles Martel to celebrate to-day or the deliverance of the Christian world, and the probable result would have been that delineated by Gibbon: "A victorious line of march had prolonged above a thousand miles, from the Rock of Gibraltar to the banks of the Loire; the repetition of an equal space would have carried the Saracens to the confines of Poland and the Highlands of Scotland; the Rhine is not more impassable than the Nile or Euphratus, and the Arabian fleet might have sailed without a naval combat into the Thames. Perhaps the interpretation of the Koran would now be taught in the schools of Oxford, and her pulpits might demonstrate to a circumcised people the sanctity and truth of the revelations of Mohammed."

In 823 the Arabs from Spain conquered Crete, and when one hundred and thirty-eight years afterward it was reconquered by Nikephorus II. (Phokas), that prince found it so thoroughly Mohammedanized that it required a new evangelization before the island could be retained for Hellenism and Christianity.

"The terrible example of the work wrought by the Arabs," says Bikelas, "in this instance is a sufficient proof of how great was the danger from which not only the Hellenic world of the East in particular, but also Christian Europe in general was saved by the efforts of the Byzantine emperors."

The power of the caliphs, however, was broken; they gave way to a new mortal foe of Christianity—that new enemy was the Turk.

In 1068 the Turks invaded the provinces of the empire and took the emperor, Romanus II., prisoner. Twenty years later they conquered Asia Minor and expelled the caliphs from Jerusalem.

The capture of the Holy City by the Turks was the cause of the crusades, which, instead of achieving the permanent deliverance of the holy places, effected the impoverishment and ruin of the Byzantine Empire.

The struggle between the empire and the Ottoman Turks lasted for four hundred years. The effort of the Turks was, by continued and violent incursions, to exterminate, if possible, the Christian inhabitants of the country, and thus weaken it, with a view to ultimate conquest. As a matter of fact, by dint of habitually massacring the peasantry, making slaves of the survivors, and reducing the cultivated tracts to a wilderness, they succeeded after a while in extinguishing the Greek population and doing away with the Greek language in the interior of Asia Minor. The imperial armies, ever becoming feebler, strove in vain to repel these sudden invasions and to protect the territory and subjects of the empire. Nevertheless, the internal dissensions among the Turks were so serious, and their wars against the Mongols so unfortunate, that it is possible the Byzantines might in the end have prevailed over them, had the Latin Christians been willing to become the allies and helpers of Christendom in the East. Unfortunately the Latins, instead of becoming allies, became enemies.

Says Bikelas, from whom I have quoted so much: "Blinded by religious and commercial rivalries, by the question of Papal supremacy, and by the material interests of the Italian republics, Western Europe failed to see that the line of defence which was imperilled was really her own, and that by being themselves the first to rend and degrade the imperial purple, the crusaders were only hastening the moment when the Turks should trample it down in mire and blood.

"Thus it came to pass that the Eastern Empire ultimately fell before the unceasing attacks of its Asiatic foes. Equally unceasing was its strife with the enemies who assailed it from the north and west. In the case of these latter, however, there always existed the tie of the common profession of the Christian religion, which always left open the door, in some sort, for the hope of reconciliation. On the other side it was quite different. Between Constantinople, Christian, Hellenic and Imperial on the one hand, and the despotism of pagan or Mohammedan Asia on the other, there was a great gulf fixed. With them no community of life could ever be possible. The Arabs took the place of the Persians, and the Turks took the place of the Arabs. From the beginning to the end the Asiatic enemy, whoever it was, was always inspired by an intense feeling of religious hatred; the motive, a rabid longing to annihilate that Christian state which formed a barrier between them and the destruction of Europe. But it was due to that barrier that Christian Europe was saved from extermination through persecution conducted by Persian fire-worshippers, and from slavery consequent on the propagation of the religion of the Koran by the sword of the Arabs. And thus it was, thanks to that barrier, that Western Europe had the time given her so to develop her strength that long after Constantinople herself had fallen in the struggle, a martyr in the cause of the human race, she was able to shatter the Turkish navies upon the waters of the Lepanto and to rout their hordes before the walls of Vienna. Unhappily, however, the fall of Constantinople was in great part the work of that very

Europe which owed and owes her so much. It is true that the deathblow was given by the battle-axe of Mahomet II., and this blow was only fatal because the victim was already half dead, but it is the crusades which are responsible more than anything else for reducing her to that condition."

In our school-books the crusades bear indeed a very different aspect. But here is the powerful truth expressed from a Greek point of view. From the facts as given by Bikelas we learn how evil may spring from the best motives. A like illustration may be given from the life of Christopher Columbus, the devout Christian. He had the idea of selling the natives of the New World as slaves in order to raise money for a new crusade. Columbus and the Knights of the Cross—the latter called themselves champions of the faith and murdered priests of Christ on the ground that they were schismatics—had views of the Christian religion which appear most peculiar now.

The appearance of the crusaders upon the stage of history is the first act in the final tragedy of the empire. The climax was reached in the capture and ransacking of Constantinople in 1204. From this outrage the empire never again rallied. "If," says Paparregopoulos, speaking of the first crusade, "the Emperor Alexis had been able to employ against the Turks the land and sea forces which he at length found himself compelled to turn against his pretended allies, and the troops which he had been obliged to send with them into Asia Minor and Syria; if he had been able to reserve for the struggle against Mohammedanism the resources of which he was plundered by the looting and extortions of the crusaders, he would have been able to get rid of all danger from the unbelievers far more effectively than was done by the ephemeral success of the Latins."

History has yet to treat the attitude of the crusaders in the East from a point of view of judicial impartiality. The images of these events are still shown to us through the glass of Western prejudices. "The Latins," says Finlay, "would not allow that their disasters were caused by their own misconduct and imprudence, they persisted in attributing all their misfortunes to the treachery of the Greeks; and though Alexis delivered many from captivity, the crusaders generally regarded him as an enemy. According to these accounts, it was always the Byzantines who were in the wrong; they were liars and traitors; and had no cause to regard the crusaders with suspicion."

The Latin conquerors remained in possession of the imperial throne for only fifty-seven years. During that time a succession of gallant emperors gathered together in exile the now recovering forces of Greek nationalism, and turned them upon the Christian adversaries until the day came in 1261, when Michael VIII. reconquered the city of Constantinople. From that time the division between the Greek and the Latin church became more marked—all attempts at reunion have thus far failed.

The Frank occupation of Greece proper which followed the seizure of Constantinople in 1204 lasted two centuries, but it has left hardly any abiding trace, and introduced no important change in the destiny of the country. Neither did it do anything to retard the progress of the Turkish conquest. And then Constantinople fell and the whole Hellenic world passed into Turkish slavery. Western Europe looked with unconcern at the appalling catastrophe.

Thus perished Constantinople, Christian and Imperial, after having fought more than a thousand years.

It was in the centuries of the Byzantine Empire that the Hellenic world which exists to-day, the New, the Christian Hellas, was formed. The decline and fall of the Greeks were not due to any fault in the people. They lacked no quality which renders states great. They met the attacks from without manfully so long as the empire had sufficient strength left to stand. The empire fell at last, exhausted, conquered, but not dishonored; it fell like a soldier who dies on the field of battle, with his sword in his hand and his face to the enemy.

Despite the many wars with their alarming situations and their dangers, Constantinople studied, worked, and continued industrious. In the midst of attacks by barbarians she preserved the traditions of the culture of Athens and Rome and prepared the way for the European Renaissance.

The fine arts developed, as we all know, with great fecundity: the Byzantines created a style of art which is known by their name. It is necessary to mention only the church of St. Sophia which has served as a model for church edifices in Italy and Russia. The predecessors and the teachers of Raphael were imitators, copyists of the Byzantines.

In Constantinople, says Finlay, manners were

milder, more Christianlike, more chaste than those of the contemporary Occident.

"The Byzantines," says Bikelas, "have, during peace and war, virtues which would have been ornamental even to old Greece. In rendering justice to these virtues which have been calumniated, in revenging their memory which has been insulted, we must confess that their noble deeds never will inflame our hearts to the same degree as will the deeds of Marathon and Plataia; our admiration for the Byzantine heroes and sages will never be that felt for the great men of antique Hellas. Is it because the Parthenon is more beautiful than St. Sophia, or because Athens was the great place of Æschylus and Thucydides, while Byzantium gave us only Photius? No; it is because Byzantium does not elevate our soul, does not inflame our hearts to the same degree as ancient Greece, because it had not the double love for *country* and *liberty*." Herein lies the difference between the two worlds which otherwise present so many analogies. Greece of to-day always has its eyes upon the glory of the Greece of the past. The national song does not invoke Constantine the Great, nor Heraclius, nor the Komnenes, nor the last of the Palæologes: the Greeks bend their knees before the memory of the three hundred of Thermopylæ when they celebrate their liberty.

> Ἀπ' τὰ κόκκαλα 'βγαλμένη
> Τῶν 'Ελλήνων τὰ ἱερά
> Καὶ 'σαν πρῶτα ἀνδρειωμένη
> Χαῖρε ὦ! χαῖρ' 'Ελευθερία

O liberty, descended from the Greeks of old and on fire with the ancient valor, hail, all hail!

And after all, alongside of the incomparable glory of the old Hellas, there lives in the grateful memory of Hellas to-day the glory of the Byzantine Greeks. The Greece of Heraclius, of Nikophorus, and of the Komnenes was in a more difficult situation than the Greece of Miltiades and Themistocles. After Marathon and Salamis Athens was delivered from the barbarians. Constantinople during ten centuries was constantly under arms against invasions. A Xerxes more terrible than the one of Herodotus appeared in every century. Athens could not have erected the Parthenon, built the long walls, applauded Sophocles, heard Pericles and Demosthenes, if Plataia had not established security for two centuries. The Greeks of to-day are bound to feel affection for the old empire. It fought long, and did not fall without glory. The devotion of the last of the Palæologs—in our time emperors do not sacrifice themselves—stands well alongside of the devotion of Leonidas. The poets of the hymn of liberty may well reverence the memory of the three hundred who died for liberty, but the poets of the Greek people have by no means forgotten Constantine Dragazes, the autocrat who sacrificed himself for his country.

Suddenly at two o'clock during the night of Tuesday, the 29th of May, 1453, began the last fight, the death agony of the Byzantines. While throughout the city the alarm bells of all the churches were ringing, and while in the churches themselves the women lay prostrate before the altars in fervent prayers of despair, the Greeks and Latins succeeded fortunately in warding off the first charge of the Osmans. The second attack, accompanied by the sound of kettle-drums and directed against the Romanos gate where the emperor himself was commanding, was likewise repulsed, with heavy losses to the Osmans. Futile also were the efforts of the marine soldiers along the docks. Then at last Mohammed ordered his best troops, the janizaries, to the attack which was preceded and sustained by the terrific fire of the largest pieces of artillery. Still the besieged stood firm, although the combat repeatedly wavered dangerously, and the number of Turks in action was seventy thousand. The Turks had already sustained severe losses, when the brave Guistiniani was seriously wounded by an arrow. The pain caused him to lose his presence of mind; he ran toward the port to have his wound dressed on board of his vessel. The confusion among the Byzantines brought on by this casualty was at once taken advantage of by Saganos Pasha; it enabled a number of the janizaries to gain a foothold upon the top of the walls, and while a fierce engagement with these janizaries was fought upon the wall, a Turkish company entered through a small gate south of the Hebdomon, which port had been opened on May 27th for the purpose of a sortie, and to the great misfortune of the Byzantines had not been locked again. They marched upon the walls in the direction of the gate of Adrianople, where they were soon reinforced by an additional force which had climbed up by the aid of ladders, and finally attacked the emperor from the rear. Now all was lost. After the Turkish cannon at the point of the principal engagement near the Romanos and Charsios gates had made a large breach in the walls, the victors entered the city without opposition. Constantine, fighting like an ordinary soldier, sought and found the *death of a hero*. The Turks for a long time massacred the Byzantine soldiers until, convinced of the numerical weakness of their adversaries, they stayed the slaughter in order to commence plundering.

A most mournful fate befell the many thousands of both sexes, of all ages, of all ranks of society, who from six to seven in the morning, since the first fatal news had been spread in the city, had fled into the church of St. Sophia. The victors broke in the doors with axes, violated boys and virgins, broke and soiled the sacred vessels, ate and drank, fed their horses, and commenced to destroy the beauty of the marvellous edifice.

The corpse of the Emperor Constantine was searched for and recognized. The Sultan ordered its head cut off and exposed on the point of a lance until evening. The trunk was permitted to be interred with imperial honors. Near the Wifa Mosque, covered by a stone without inscription under a laurel tree, is the tomb of the noble hero; above it a simple lamp, supplied with oil, is lit every evening.

CHAPTER IV.

THE GREEKS UNDER TURKISH BONDAGE.

THE monstrous wrong had been accomplished; the old magnificent city of Constantine the Great was now in the hands of the ruler of the Osmans. A history of eleven centuries had reached its termination. The significance of the increase of power of the Turks was soon apparent to the Christian nations of the West, who had permitted the last Emperor of Byzantium to perish.

As the history of the Hellenes during the last century of the Roman republic belongs to the dark leaves in the annals of the Greek people, exactly so does the history of this nation from the time of the appearance of the fearful Mohammed II. present for centuries a dark picture, only scantily illuminated here and there by a flash of light.

We have to place ourselves in a certain far-distant position to obtain a historical perspective in order to see how the subjection and the gathering of the whole Greek nation under Osmanic government secured for the Greeks the possibility of remaining a united nation until this day. The union under the Osmanic rule was due in the first instance to the gradual destruction of all the Frankish rulers on Greek soil, and in the second place to the misrule of the Turks, which, being to all Greeks worse than death, made them risk their lives in a struggle for liberty.

Western Europe for centuries forgot the existence of a Greek people; not so the Osmans.

The unfortunate Greek people, for centuries excluded from all active participation in politics, living only as members of their respective communities, did not enjoy the modest satisfaction of being enabled to accumulate wealth.

The Turks had only one thing in view in regard to the Greeks: to govern and to tax them. According to Turkish law the Sultan was the real owner of all conquered soil. The vast majority of the Greek peasants were therefore simply tenants or common laborers.

The Greeks had to pay the kharadsh; furthermore they were obliged to contribute a tenth, which in reality meant often as much as a fifth or even a third, of all that they raised or produced *in natura;* they had also to pay rent, and if this were not enough, they had to do soccage service, and to all this was added the most infernal blood tribute of which we shall speak presently.

In exhausting the conquered land by extortion the Turks acted like animals with thoughtless instinct; they ate what they found without thinking of the next day. "Wherever," observes the English eye-witness Eton, "the Turks have established their dominion, science and commerce, the comforts and the knowledge of mankind have alike decayed. Not only have they exemplified barbarism and intolerance in their own conduct, but they have extinguished the flame of genius and knowledge in others." Higher aims in regard to literature, science, and art did not exist among the Turks, not even music was cultivated. Since the Turks are polygamists they are without that institution, monogamy, which more than anything else is apt to coerce animal passion in man. Even those who understand the Turks best and judged them mildly had to confess that the lower classes were ignorant, lazy, fanatic; that the upper classes, as a rule, appeared dull from debauch, most of the time brooding and smoking after exhaustion from sensual excesses.

Turkish government means destruction of

public welfare and prosperity. Bikelas writes: "In the year 1204, when Villehardouin and his fellow-comrades came into contact with the East, their first emotion was one of amazement at the spectacle of such marvellous wealth and splendor, but since those days the Turks have been allowed to effect a complete change. The travellers who visited the Turks at the end of the last or the beginning of this century are unanimous in recording with horror the wretchedness which was coextensive with the Ottoman Empire. The inhabitants had learned by experience not even to till the ground beyond what was necessary for the bare support of life." "They have no courage," says the French traveller Savary, "no spirit. And why should they attempt anything? If they took to sowing or planting, it would lead to the idea that they were rich, and so inevitably bring down the aga to devour whatever they possess." The cultivators of the soil and the manufacturers, all exposed to the extortions from public officers, lived in constant anxiety and fear. For this reason most fertile land, perhaps nine-tenths of all, remained uncultivated. Where the densest population might have lived in abundance, the smallest one had to contend with famine. There was no systematic administration, no protection against conflagration, against inundation, there was no provision made for good roads, there existed no precaution against the plague and other epidemics. Foreign relations grew less and less "on account," as is expressed by M. Chaptal, "of the insecurity which reigns inland, where every species of disorder was rampant." "Our own French merchants," says M. Juchereau de Saint-Denis, "were at one with those of Holland and England in complaining, years before our revolution, that trade in the Levant had ceased to offer the same advantages as formerly, and they attributed the miserable prices offered for their own merchandise and the diminution of their profits to the increasing poverty and depopulation of the Turkish Empire." The plain of Elis had become an uncultivated wilderness. "The execrable government of the Morea," says the English witness Leake, "added to local tyranny, has reduced the Greeks of Gastouni to such distress that all the cultivated land is now in the hands of the Turks, and the Greek population have become cattle feeders or mere laborers for the Turkish possessors of the soil."

With the cessation of cultivation and production ceased also the communication with the rest of the world. Greece became unknown. From time to time travellers like those already quoted would venture to visit Hellas to see what monuments of her past greatness might still survive. Some of these men were moved by sympathy; others reproached the unfortunate Greeks, cruelly and unjustly, as being unworthy of the soil of classical Hellas. And even this very day those latter sentiments run riot in the heads of a large class of ignorant and malevolent people, and in anti-Hellenic literature. "When I was at Gastouni," says M. Bartholdy, "I overheard a conversation between an English traveller, a Greek monk, and our host, who was the doctor in the place. The churchman and the physician complained bitterly of the Turkish yoke. 'God,' said the Englishman, 'has deprived the Hellenes of their freedom because they did not deserve to have it.'" "The town of Dhivri," says the traveller Leake, already quoted, "occupies a large space, the houses to the number of three hundred being dispersed in clusters over the side of the hills, but a great part of them are uninhabited. This is chiefly owing to the angária of the Lalliotes, who come here and force the poor Greeks to carry straw, wood, without payment." The inhabitants of Monembasia and its neighborhood had endeavored to save themselves by emigrating to Hydra, to Spezzia, and even to Asia Minor. Different travellers tell of deserted villages and districts in Morea. Greeks went to Asia Minor where they were subject only to the land tax and the kharadsh. The poor wretches by nomadic movements, as Bikelas says, "strove to find some amelioration in their condition by passing from one part to another of the Ottoman Empire." This was merely like the action of a sick man who seeks to find relief by thrusting his aching limbs first into one and then into another part of his bed of pain. "The depopulation of some provinces," testifies M. Juchereau de Saint-Denis, "has been so marked that, out of twenty flourishing villages which formerly existed in the neighborhood of Aleppo, it is now scarcely possible to reckon four or five. The tyranny of the provincial governors drives the peasants to seek refuge in the town, and, once they are there, starvation soon decimates them."

Wealth, whether honestly or dishonestly accumulated, was a danger to its possessor; even the Sultan would lie in wait, and still much more the pashas who had bought their offices and acted in their provinces like hungry wolves. All offices had to be bought; even the Sultan sold the highest offices to the highest bidder. Frederick the Great said the Turks would sell even their prophets for money. Felix Beaujour, a traveller, says: "The whole divan is for sale, if only the intending purchaser has money enough wherewith to buy it; and this is the reason why the beys and the agas utilize the provinces to obtain the means of saving themselves from the bowstring and acquiring appointments to the office of pasha. They buy their appointments at Constantinople, where there is nothing which is not for sale, and they recoup themselves any way they can. Throughout the whole of the Ottoman Empire the governors work an inexhaustible mine of fines." This system extinguished all honor in public offices, and encouraged extortion. Judges as well as witnesses could be bought and bribed. A man who might have been honest in private life could not help being tainted with corruption and dishonesty when connected with the public service. The sense of duty and right upon which all public welfare depends was wanting.

It was the habit of the pasha to make a periodical round of all the towns and villages under his jurisdiction, in order to receive the "voluntary offerings" of his wretched subjects. When

"Ali," says Leake, "makes a tour round this part of his territory, he never fails to visit this place. The archons generally meet him in the plains, and offer perhaps twenty purses, begging him not to come into town. He receives the present with smiles, promises that he will not put his friends to inconvenience; afterward comes a little nearer, informs them that no provisions are to be had in the plain, and, after being supplied upon the promise of not entering the town, quarters on them, in the course of a day or two more, with his whole suite, perhaps for several days, and he does not retire until he has received a fresh donation. In these rounds he expects something from every village, and will accept the smallest offerings from individuals. His sons, in travelling, do not fail to follow so great an example. . . . Neither pestilence nor famine is more dreaded by the poor natives than the arrival of these little scraps of coarse paper scrawled with a few Greek characters, and stamped with the well-known seal which makes Epirus, Thessaly, and Macedonia tremble."

The people of Galaxidi had taken flight because Ali Pasha wished to compel them to serve as sailors on board the fleet which he was equipping.

"The present pasha of the Morea," says Leake, "is said to have paid the Porte four hundred purses for his appointment for one year, and he will probably squeeze one thousand out of the poor province. Vanli Pasha, who was removed last year to Candia, paid six hunderd purses for two years, and yet greatly enriched himself. The Morea has the character of being the most profitable pashalik in the empire."

In the report which Capodistria addressed in 1828 to the representatives of the powers in answer to the questions which they had put to his Government, he gives some extremely interesting information as to the manner in which pashas were in the habit of exercising their powers: "How was it possible," he asks, "to look for just and enlightened administration from a pasha who but very shortly before attaining that dignity had been employed as a slaughterman, and who is now simply the ignorant nominee of an absolute despot? . . . No man dared to open his mouth in the presence of the pasha of the Peloponnesos. That pasha had the power of life and death over his subjects, and they trembled whenever they had to go near his seraglio. Fear seized them before even they found themselves within sight of the despot, or within earshot of the terrors of his voice. At the gate of his palace were always to be found ready waiting a hundred and fifty soldiers under full arms, an itch-aga, and an executioner. It needed only a significant move of his head to cause any one of his petitioners to be led out to die."

"The Ottoman Empire," says Pouqueville, "is the empire of woe. It is not like any other country in the world. The people who live in it are at once ferocious and apathetic, and are destitute of the slightest feeling for the public interest. From Constantinople to the banks of the Euphratus, and from the shores of the Bosphorus to Cattaro, the towns are cesspools full of dung and filth, the villages are either dens of wild beasts or deserted. The exclusive subjects of conversation are pestilence, conflagrations, epidemics, and famines. The gates of the great cities are hidden by groups of gibbets, and towers loaded with human skulls. The roads traversed by the local governors are lined with gory heads, stakes for impalement, and other instruments of death. The traveller meets no one who is not clad in the livery of destitution. There is no police, no public order, no rest, and no safety for life and property. The gentler virtues are unknown in this country. If a man has money he buries it, and if he has any valuable objects he hides them in the depths of his harem. If he wishes to escape suspicion he must avoid living with the appearance of being in easy circumstances."

Savary relates an anecdote illustrating the treatment the Greeks received in their own country. The circumstances occurred in 1780. With the exception of the archbishop and of Europeans, no Christian has the right to ride inside a town. The Bishop of Canea took it in his head to disregard this tyrannical regulation. One evening, when he was returning from the country along with several monks, he did not dismount, but passed through and rode quickly up to his own house. The janizaries who were on guard at the gate looked on this action as an insult. The next day they roused the troops, and it was determined to burn the bishop and the priests. The mob, roaring curses, were already carrying combustibles to the bishop's house, and its inhabitants could not have escaped the horrible fate to which they were destined, had not the pasha, warned in time, issued a proclamation, by which any Greek, of what class soever, was forbidden to sleep within the walls of Canea. This prohibition was rigorously enforced, and every evening these wretched slaves might be seen slinking out of the gates of Rettimo, and retiring for the night into the fields. This state lasted for two months, but money is here the cure for all evils. The Cretans collected their resources together, and by a very heavy bribe, obtained the revocation of the verdict. The pride of their bishop cost them dear.

Eton relates: "The insulting distinction of Christian and Mohammedan is carried to so great a length that even the minutiæ of dress are rendered subjects of restriction. A Christian must wear clothes and head-dresses of dark colors only, and such as Turks never wear, with slippers of black leather, and must paint his house black or dark brown. The least violation of these frivolous and disgusting regulations is punished with death."

A Christian on horseback had to dismount as soon as he came in sight of a Turk. The government of the Sublime Porte invented with great ingenuity infinite humiliations and vexations for the Greeks, for objects of taxation. Churches could not be built nor repaired without conditional payment of large sums to a mosque at Constantinople; sometimes the sums demanded were exorbitant.

If a neighborhood happened to possess any natural peculiarity, this feature was taken advantage of for the benefit of the Turks. There is a spot near Kandelion in the Peloponnesus, where the snow lies long. "The mountain on the left," says Leake, "has a remarkable cavern, or a shady hollow, an unlucky circumstance for the poor Kandeliotes, who are obliged to supply the serail at Tripoliza from it, and carry the snow there at their own expense."

Any Turk could with impunity maltreat a Christian. Colonel Leake saw a Turk kill a Greek peasant at the gate of Larissa, because the Christian had an ass loaded with charcoal, which he wished to carry for sale to the market place in hopes of a more certain, as well as a higher price for it, instead of letting the Turks have it. It is hardly necessary to add, says Bikelas, in whose lectures all the reports of travellers here enumerated are collected, that the Cadi declared the murderer guiltless. The only chance of a conviction would have been, if the family of the victim had had more money. However, it was not held to be a crime for a Turk to murder a Christian.

Christians were not admitted as witnesses against Turks. If, however, Christians were wealthy they could buy Turkish witnesses, who were never wanting to call God to witness to anything so long as a suitor was able and willing to pay them to do so. If the suitor possessed the funds which were needed for securing the favor of the judge his case stood very well.

We will not go into details in regard to Turkish jurisprudence, which was obscure and often inconsistent. Capodistria has given an account of it in the statement already mentioned. "It may be remarked," says Eton, "that there is not one instance of a fetra which declares the murder of a Christian to be contrary to the faith; or of any argument drawn from justice or religion, used to dissuade the sultans from perpetrating such an enormity. But, on the other hand," remarks the same writer, "a Christian may not kill a Mohammedan even in self-defence; if a Christian only strikes a Mohammedan, he is most commonly put to death on the spot, or at least ruined by fines and severely bastinadoed; if he strikes, though by accident, a sheriff (emil in Turkish, *i.e.*, a descendant of Mohammed, who wears green turbans), of whom there are thousands in the cities, it is death without remission."

We learn from Olivier that in Crete the Turks are more than anywhere else given, upon the slightest pretext, to either killing a Greek with their own hands or sending him to execution.

The most convenient medium for the extortions of the Turkish governors was the kharadsh. Every raya, says Eton, that is, every subject who is not of the Mohammedan religion) is allowed only the cruel alternative of death or tribute, capitation tax. The very words of the formula given to the Christian subjects paying the kharadsh, or capitation tax, import that the sum of money received is taken as a compensation for being *permitted to wear their heads that year*.

Mohammedan jurisprudence recognizes between Mohammedan and non-Mohammedan nations but one category of relations—that of djehâd or holy war. By the sacred law all giaours (Christian dogs) are under the ban. Yet, although devoted to destruction, they may be spared for a season, whenever this is to the advantage of Islam. That these principles of law are in force in Turkey to this very day is fully shown in a most scientific article by Professor A. D. F. Hamlin which appeared in *The Forum*, July, 1897. This paper of Professor

Hamlin furnishes conclusive evidence that the above reports from travellers in Greece during the time of the Turkish bondage are by no means exaggerations or inventions.

It is one of the strangest occurrences that books are published and journals appear which deny or make little of the ill treatment the Greeks were subjected to by the Turks. Such whitewashing was done for political ends during the time of the Greek war of independence, and many writers of to-day either do not or will not search for historical truth.

The nominal figure, says Bikelas, of the poll tax was not high. But the collectors, to whom the collection was sublet, always found means for extorting from the taxpayers at least double the sum which found its way into the treasury. The fifty per cent went, as a matter of course, into their own pockets. Even children of eight years in towns and five in the country were assessed. If, says Beaujour, the father of a little Greek raises any dispute as to his exact age, the tax gatherers measure the child's head with a cord, which is made to serve as a sort of a standard, and, as they can make the cord what length they like, the father can always be proved in the wrong.

In the islands it was in vain that inhabitants fled to their mountains when the tax collectors came. The Turks seized the elders and put them to the bastinado until their wives had brought them their trinkets and those of the neighboring women. It was, moreover, very often the case that the Turks, after appropriating the jewelry, threw husband, wife, and child into slavery. Besides, the inhabitants of the isles were subject to a blood tax, conscription of young men for service in the Turkish fleet.

Yet the conscription, writes Bikelas, of seafaring lads was as nothing in comparison with that indescribable blood tax, the conscription of little children, the memory of which haunts every Greek home like the presence of a devil. Every five years came the moment when the Greek nation received a stab into the heart, when a tenth in human flesh was taken, a tenth which deprived the people of the hope based on the blossom of the manly youth, and which desolated the land with most atrocious certainty. Small detachments of Turkish soldiers, each detachment commanded by a captain and each armed with a special firman, travelled through the provinces from place to place. When they came the elders of the villages or towns gathered the inhabitants

THE GREEKS UNDER TURKISH BONDAGE. 149

with their sons. The Turkish officer had the power to seize one-fifth of all the boys between the age of seven years and puberty and to select those who were especially handsome, strong, and intelligent or otherwise talented. The fathers and mothers knew that the children they lost were lost to them forever, that they would be circumcised, become Mohammedans, live and die janizaries. As for the race, this tribute threatened its very existence, the very hope of its future was turned against it, its persecutors forged from its very blood the instruments of their oppression. No other enslaved nation has ever had to suffer such torture as this.

With all these historical facts before us, it would be difficult to understand how writers, as for instance W. Alison Phillips in a book recently published and entitled "The War of Greek Independence, 1821 to 1833" (New York: Charles Scribner's Sons, 1897), can repeat statements like the following, did not the author give us the explanation: "It is a mistake to suppose that it was the intolerable tyranny of the Turk which forced the Greeks into rebellion." "In many parts of the Turkish dominions, the cultivators of the soil enjoyed a prosperity unknown to the peasantry of some nations accounted more civilized." He enumerates the books from which he has taken his information. He has selected just those which were either written in an anti-Hellenic spirit or which do not contain the researches of those historians of our time who have made real scientific investigations. Thus, for instance, he does not or will not know the writings of Zinkeisen, Ross, Gervinus, Bikelas, and the excellent historian Hertzberg. On the other hand he has used a book, as he confesses himself, which was issued by its author as a counterblast to the Armenian agitation, intended as an apology for the Turk and an indictment of the Oriental Christian. Mr. Phillips, it appears, has never heard of the horrible blood tax of which mention is made above, or is it that he does not wish to state anything which is unfavorable to the Turk? I refer to this author only because his book is the most recent on hand, and it will serve as an example of how some writers treat modern Greek history, namely, by misrepresentation, by omission, and by repetition of old intentional untruths.

But, to return to the horrors of the Turkish reign over the Greeks: The proverb says where there is much light there is much shadow. Here we may say, where there is so much shadow there must be some light. And indeed we shall now see the dawn of a new glory of Hellas, when we come to speak of her great patriot Koraïs, and further on when we shall see how their religion was the most potent means of saving the Greeks.

Koraïs, in the preface to his translation of Beccaria, expressed his conviction that no remedy could heal the misfortune of the Greeks but the light of science; and he made it his task to imbue the hearts of the youth of Hellas with love for their glorious ancestors, the youth who were destined to become Greece's legislators.

From the moment Koraïs read his "Memoire sur l'état actuel de la civilisation dans la Grèce" before a learned society in Paris in 1803, in order to direct the eyes of the world to the regeneration of his country, until the time of the uprising of the Greeks, when he wrote his political admonitions, he incessantly reminded his countrymen of patriotism, union, lawfulness, and perseverance. He spoke to them as citizen, as patriot, as philosopher, in the spirit of Plutarch, who wrote his biographies for the purpose of giving the oppressed Greeks self-respect before the Romans. Koraïs' aim all the time was to convince his countrymen that the political resurrection of Greece had to be prepared by means of spiritual regeneration, and as a corollary that the spiritual regeneration would positively be followed by political resurrection. He implored them in the name of the Fatherland, of wife and child, of God and religion, of all that was sacred to the Greeks, of the graves of father and mother, that the people should rise against the barbaric oppressors who had robbed them of law and morals and honor, of life and faith and virtue.

Koraïs' opinions and views were shared by a large number of travellers who, as we have related already, visited Greece in the beginning of this century, men of excellent character, and with sound, profound judgment.

Every change in the fate of the Greek people, every political movement of theirs had its reflex on the rest of Europe. During the fifteenth century, as we have seen, when the conquest of the Osmans forced Greek scholars to disperse, they united with the humanists, and this memorable union brought about a revival of Greek learning in the schools of the Western world. When in the seventeenth century Crete was taken by the Turks Europe regretted to see all places of classical Greece in the hands of the barbarians. When in the eighteenth century Russification of Greece was threatening, it created a shudder in the world of learning throughout Europe. The many publications of French and English travellers at the end of the eighteenth and the beginning of this century show the deep interest the people of those countries had in the fate of Greece.

After Koraïs in Paris had begun to make comparisons between old and new Hellas, men of learning of all nationalities vied with each other to instruct the Greeks in their own history; after Koraïs, the great Greek scholar, had visited Europe and made himself heard there, men of science went to Greece.

The first in time and the first in value of these travellers was Colonel William Martin Leake, the celebrated English archæologist, born in 1777. He came of a high family, was an officer of the British artillery, and lived in the Levant, being entrusted with a diplomatic mission, from 1804-9. In 1823 he received his discharge as lieutenant-colonel and thereafter devoted his time to science and the publication of his writings. These publications show profound critical judgment, power of practical observation, extensive learning in geography, history, and literature, and unsurpassed clearness of diction in the description of the conditions of ancient as well as modern Hellas. The rich information which he had gained by his travels in almost all parts of Greece are found in his works: "Travels in the Morea," 3 vols., London, 1830; "Travels in Northern Greece," 4 vols., Cambridge, 1835; "Topography of Athens," 2 vols., second edition, Cambridge, 1841; "Tour in Asia Minor," London, 1824; "Memoir on the Island of Cos," London, 1843; "Greece at the End of Twenty-three Years of Protection," London, 1851. Having finished his elaborate work, "Numismatica Hellenica," 3 vols., Cambridge, 1854–59, he died January 6th, 1860, at Brighton.

Other travellers were W. Gell, Dodwell, Douglas, Lord Guildford, Macdonald, Kinneir, Holland, Hughes, Hobhouse, Byron. Athens was at that time the meeting-place for strangers, a regular colony of scholars. The central figure in this society was for a time Lord Guildford, whom the Greeks gave the name of the greatest, the three times greatest Philhellene. There was also the Austrian Consul Gropius, a Philhellene, notwithstanding the pronounced hatred of his government toward the Greeks. Further the Frenchman Fauval, who for a period of thirty years was looked upon and honored as the custos of the ruins.

While all the fearful destruction was going on in Greece the Acropolis of Athens had not been completely ruined. It appears as if even the barbarians had been charmed by the divine art. The edifice would have been much better preserved if Christian hands had not contributed to its ruin: the Venetian siege in 1687, Greek defence during the war of independence, and English vandalism. Lord Elgin, recalled from his post as ambassador to Constantinople, passed through Greece, and with Turkish permission deprived the temple of Minerva of its most beautiful ornament. All foreigners, foremost the Frenchmen, and even many Englishmen— Lord Byron more than anybody else—were furious in their condemnation of such vandalism. The most touching reproach is contained in the Athenian tale: When one of the five Caryatides of the pandrosium was taken away the other four girls in the evening cried after their lost sister with painful woe, and the one who had been taken away answered them from the lower part of the city with similar cries of pain.

The number of foreign guests increased. They all were filled with compassion when they observed the dull silence of slavery, and men like Chateaubriand in their writings awakened sympathy, drawing the hearts from the ruins of stone to the living ruins. It is impossible to understand how any one could look upon the cruel treatment of this people without being touched, how any one could wander without heartfelt pity among these oppressed unfortunates in a country where there is no stone without a name, no brook, no spring which has not been celebrated in poetry or history, where every ravine, every valley reminds one of great deeds and great men. Foreign wanderers on this soil voluntarily hoped for and dreamed of the resurrection of Greece. To many it appeared as if the jealousy of the powers, which regarded Turkey as a necessary barrier against Russia, delayed the day of Greece's liberty. Most of them, however, agreed with Koraïs that the intellectual activity of the Greeks would be the forerunner of this complete resurrection, and necessarily had to be.

All travellers, even those who believed that the Greeks were so devoid of education and virtue that they could not understand and create a better political condition, deemed it cruel to see them condemned to everlasting slavery. Those who witnessed the system of outrage under which the Greeks were suffering declared it shameful that civilized nations allowed the Turks continually to oppress this people.

The American Revolution had established principles of human rights and spread democratic views.

The Greeks were found in misery, but even among the peasants who lived in out-of-the-way places there existed the feeling of shame at their ignorance. They were surprised that strangers interested themselves in their condition, approaching as it did that of animals. This spark of self-knowledge kindled hope in those who had pitied them. For there was none even among the most malevolent travellers who was not full of admiration of the activity, the desire for knowledge, the intelligence, the individual self-possession, the soundness of judgment, the practical sense, the talent of rhetoric in this people.

For political reasons, perhaps in order to accustom the Greeks to bear their yoke the better, to facilitate the control over them, the Patriarch, the ecclesiastical head, was empowered to exercise civil jurisdiction over the Christians. The Greeks were allowed the public celebration of their religious worship, the clergy were exempt from the kharadsh, and were themselves allowed to levy a tax upon every Christian family, in order to meet the expenses incidental to the discharge of their public functions. The clerics thus placed at the head of the Hellenic people showed themselves endowed with such an amount of intelligence and of patriotism that they upheld the standard of Hellenism under the shelter of the Phanar. The Greek Church never lost the consciousness of her duty toward the Greek nation. The Greek people owe to their church the preservation of their faith, of their language, and of their unity; yes, we may say, of their race. The Greeks will never be found lacking in gratitude toward their Church. Some errors from which the higher clergy had not always been free were more than atoned for by the death of the Patriarch, Gregor V., hanged at the Phanar in 1821; by the patriotic devotion of Germanus of Patras; and by the deeds of so many other prelates who have died as the martyrs or lived as the confessors of the cause of Greek national independence.

Happily amid the degradation which the national character suffered under the influence of the dangers and the evils of slavery, the Hellenic people never lost the sense of their own dignity.

It was this sense which made them long to be free again. The consciousness of dishonor hurt them more than the hardships of the life of slavery. Proofs of this exist in the writings which Hellenes published in foreign countries, and, after the war broke out, in documents in which the insurgents made known to Europe their resolve to die sooner than endure again what they had suffered so long.

Next to the privileges granted to the Church it was the communal system which was the social anchor to which Hellenism owed its preservation. While the patriarchs supplied the elements of political unity, the communal system gave shape to the home life of the people.

The pressure of slavery, which weighed upon all alike, made close the ties which bound the members of every family, of every little community together. It is needless to enter here into the question whether the communal system which existed in Greece under the Turks owed its origin to classical or mediæval times. Fortunately, it did not occur to the Turks to make any attack upon this system. On the contrary, they found that it suited their system of administration very well. Just as they made the Patriarch of Constantinople responsible for the whole race, so did they make the elders responsible for the whole of each community. It facilitated the assessing of tribute, the regulating of the forced labor, and the getting in the kharadsh.

The communal system, by binding the interests of every individual to those of institutions common to all, by concerning all in the local government, in the affairs of schools and hospitals, prepared the people for freedom. The Greeks had and have a family life more intimate and more pure than many of the people of the South; they treated their women with that respect which is due to their sex, and this alone already gave them the expectation for higher culture.

When the war of independence broke out the communal societies served as centres of activity, and also as bases for the new organization of the country. The elders of all kinds, like the prelates of the church and the rest of the Phanariote hierarchy, now cast aside the signs of their slavery and degradation and contended for the honor of leading the national movement.

When the war broke out it became more manifest how vast a gulf separated Hellene from Turk. For four centuries had they been associated in intimate contact. Mutual familiarity had only intensified their mutual hatred. The

Turk degraded and corrupted the Greek population, and the Osmanic government looked upon all Hellenes as enemies, and treated them accordingly.

Bikelas has shown in a special treatise how large a part of the awakening of the Greeks was due to the increase of education. In the earlier periods of Ottoman dominion education was confined to a few clergy and a still more limited number of laymen. The mass of the population was plunged into ignorance. The village teacher was generally the parish priest, and the few pupils whom he could gather around him acquired little more than a mechanical power of reading the Psalms and the ecclesiastical office books. From the seventeenth century the Hellenes in the service of the Porte rendered aid to the Patriarchate in commencing an extended system of education, by founding schools, and protecting the teachers and their pupils. The true development, however, took place toward the end of the last century. Then it was that the lowly teachers of the preceding generations gave place to men of learning with love for the classical glory of their race. Thenceforth many a Hellenic town had a school, and pupils came from the country round about. In these schools, moreover, the works of classical authors and of the fathers of the Church no longer formed the only subjects of study. In them were taught the results of modern science, either from original works or from translations of the best foreign treatises.

The principal source, says Bikelas, which supplied means to education, and was the strongest lever for raising the Greek people out of the rut of lethargy into which they had fallen, was commerce. Commercial activity dates its revival from the eighteenth century.

The Greeks of other days, said M. Juchereau de Saint-Denis, crushed under the yoke of Osmanic despotism, used to get European merchandise through the medium of European agents, established in the different seaports of the Levant. Within the last fifty years, under the impulse of their constantly disappointed hopes for a brighter future, they have taken to studying our language, imitating some of our manners and customs, and trying to gain some knowledge of Europe by personal observation. From the epoch when he wrote, the commerce of the Levant became mainly centred in the hands of the Hellenes. The Greeks began to experience pleasurable sensations of ease and comfort, and with this improvement began the aspiration after a higher position. The Greeks are more industrious than any other southern people, and under equal taxation and justice they would by their industry alone have starved out their Turkish masters. By carrying on commerce and navigation on a grand scale during the first period of their awakening, they proved themselves so much superior that the observing Englishmen, full of admiration for their talent, their perspicacity, their experience, diligence, economy, and honesty, predicted with the most absolute certainty their success. Their merchant ships were indeed now beginning, in ever-increasing number, to bear to their homes the wealth which was destined later on to keep alive the war of independence. The improvement was soon to be seen in landward Hellas also, wherever the absence of Turks permitted some security and freedom. The existence of such oases in the midst of the desert of Osmanli savagery startled the few travellers. The German Bartholdy, who was by no means favorably inclined toward the Greeks, was astonished to find at Ampelania, in Thessaly, several persons who were capable of addressing him in his mother tongue, and he was still more astonished when he found that, as a recreation, they had opened a small theatre, in which they were representing Kotzebue's "Menschenhass und Reue," which was then in vogue in civilized Europe. At Kallarrytes, at Syracon, in Epirus similar phenomena were to be found. It is the tradition of Kallarrytes, says Leake, that the Vlakhiotes have not been settled in this part of Pindus more than two hundred and fifty years, which is very credible, as it is not likely that they quitted the more fertile parts of Thessaly until they felt the oppression of the Turkish conquerors, and their inability to resist it. The removal has not been unfortunate, for their descendants have thereby enjoyed a degree of repose, and have obtained advantages which their former situation could hardly have admitted. They began by carrying to Italy the woollen cloaks, called *cappe*, which are made in these mountains and much used in Italy and in Spain, as well as by the Greeks themselves. This opened the route for a more extended commerce; they now share with the Greeks in the valuable trade of colonial produce between Spain and Malta, and many are owners of both ship and cargo. The wealthier inhabitants are merchants who have been abroad many years in Italy, Spain, or the dominions of

Austria or Russia, and who after a long absence have returned with the fruits of their industry to their native towns, which they thus enrich and in some degree civilize. But they seldom return for permanent residence till late in life, being satisfied in the interval with two or three short visits. The middle classes pursue a similar course; but, as their traffic seldom carries them as far from home as the higher order of merchants, they return more frequently, and many of them spend a part of every summer in their native place.

At Siatista, in Macedonia, Bikelas narrates, there could hardly be said to be a single family some member of which was not established in Italy, in Hungary, in Austria, or in Germany. Among the old men in the town, there were very few who had not lived abroad for ten or twelve years. Among the mountain villages near Volo, in Thessaly, the same activity was attended with the same results. It is to these merchants, while either still living in some foreign land or when returned to their native country, that Hellas owes that wonderful revival of popular education which preceded her political resurrection. Such men were Zosimai, the Maroutsoi, the Kaplanai, and so many other benefactors of their race. Such were those who founded and endowed schools. There were others who were either themselves workers in the fields of literature and learning, or who generously subsidized and supported the publication of useful books by others. These were the men who made themselves the leading apostles of freedom and of civilization, by telling their fellow-countrymen what they had heard and seen in the dominions of civilized governments, and exciting in them the desire to obtain similar blessings for their own land. It is among these merchants that are to be found the names of the first founders of the Hetairia. It was principally from among them that the emissaries were drawn who spread through the provinces and colonies of the Hellenic race the secret knowledge of the national movement which was about to break forth. Of six hundred and ninety-two recorded names of members of the Hetairia, two hundred and fifty-one are those of business men, and thirty-five of ship owners.

Bikelas concludes: Trade helped to engender the war of independence, trade brought out and hastened the moral and intellectual awakening of the people. In the merchant ships were raised those sailors who have gained immortality by fighting for Greece. The Church and the communal system had, as we have seen, saved the integrity and the unity of the nation. The klephthai and the armatoloi, from generation to generation, had handed down the warrior spirit of the Hellenic race, and when the hour of battle came Hellas had children who could fight for her.

CHAPTER V.

THE GREEK WAR OF INDEPENDENCE AND THE EUROPEAN POWERS.

FROM the time of their complete ruin the Greeks attempted to rise again. Agitations and plots existed continually. As they felt that they were not strong enough by themselves, they asked for help from the Christians of Western Europe. Different projects were set on foot for raising a new crusade. Meanwhile, however, the Greeks seized upon every occasion to break out into insurrections, which being suppressed, only served the Turks as a pretext to make slavery more severe. Charles VIII. intended to help the Greeks re-establish the Greek empire. Laskaris and Arianites were in the conspiracy to prepare a general rising of the Greeks as soon as the King of France should set foot among them. But Charles VIII. dying, the scheme was abandoned. Many other brilliant schemes and ingenious plots to resuscitate the Byzantine empire, different projects to raise a new crusade, and the insurrections which broke out in

Greece, all came to nothing. Only one of the Western European states, the republic of Venice, was incessantly opposing the Turks, and often with success, but the Venetians in their turn likewise oppressed the Greeks. They acted not as their friends, but from selfish motives.

The religious separation between the Eastern and the Western churches is a thing of great importance to be considered in regard to the position of the Greek people toward the peoples of Western Europe. This religious dissension was to some extent the reason why Western Europe ceased to care what happened to the Greeks. The Turks made their final conquests in the south; they took Crete. The last half of the seventeenth century was the direst period through which the Greeks ever had to pass.

With the beginning of the eighteenth century Greece hoped for help from Russia, the very power whose population shared her religious belief, and who freely fed her with promises and encouragements. Catharine II. together with Emperor Joseph II. both had for a time the same plans as Charles VIII.—namely, to restore the Byzantine-Greek empire. The Greeks were for the first time undeceived in their confidence in Russia at the time of the insurrection in 1770 on the appearance of the Russian fleet under Orloff. In the treaty which ended this Turko-Russian war the Greeks were entirely forgotten; they were left to the mercy of their old tyrants. The vengeance which the Turks took was terrible.

This first attempt to bring about a general rising of a whole nation, although it failed, was far from extinguishing all hope. The struggle was not given up, and the Klephtai in the mountains kept it continually alive.

The Greeks began to face the Turks at sea. Lampros Katzones fitted out about the year 1788, with the help of patriotic subscriptions, a little fleet, and the Greek banner with the cross of Christ was floating over the Greek seas until the Turks destroyed this small navy in 1792. Now the American and the French revolutions had their effect on Greece; they hastened the national awakening. Two apostles of the gospel of liberty, Rhigas and Koraïs, preached the principles of the French Revolution.

The Hetairia was a secret patriotic brotherhood, a national league, organized by Constantine Rhigas, who took the opportunity to form this union when the attention of his compatriots had been directed from the events of the French

Revolution to their own sad condition, a union which was created to prepare the way for political revolution. The first step of these united patriots was toward promotion of public instruction and education.

Rhigas, handed over by the Austrian police to the Turks, was executed by the latter in 1798, but the elements of his society remained, and it was reorganized and received new life during the years of 1814–17. Every member had the right, with the consent of another, to receive any Greek whom he believed to possess the required qualities. The new member knew only the one who had admitted him. Before admission his life's conduct, his principles, his financial circumstances were strictly examined, and on admission the candidate had to swear an oath which gave evidence of his piety, love of liberty, and patriotism. The next object was to secure contributions, which every new member, through the one who had admitted him, had to make to the national treasury. The whole was governed by a central head which had possession of the funds. To gain new members and for other purposes apostles were sent out, and in many places of the Turkish Empire, especially in Constantinople, the society had its agents and ephores.

About 1818 the Hetairia commenced to prepare the Greeks for a change of their condition to be expected in the near future. Greece was ready for liberty. All her population were but waiting the moment to shake the chains from their limbs. The apostles of the brotherhood had everywhere good ground.

When the war broke out there was a want of organization either military or political, the means were insufficient, and there was no alliance and no hope of help from any foreign nation. On the side of the Osmanli there were power and strength; the struggle was to be a desperate one. Hellas in fighting for many years against her gigantic oppressor received no quarter, her population became much more than decimated, in the field, by massacres, by epidemics. Turkish savagery spared nothing. The towns were destroyed. The country was laid waste. When all the bloodshed, the horrors of was were over, only a little fraction of the Hellenic race obtained independence. Three hundred thousand Hellenes gave up their lives in order that six hundred thousand might be free. This independence could be won only sword in hand in order to wash out the stains of slavery.

Some people thought the Greeks, instead of

taking up arms and proclaiming their rights, would have gained these rights in the course of time and events, by cabals and intrigues, perhaps peacefully. "But," says Bikelas, "to what depths of degradation would the Greek race have sunk had they refused the ancestral blood which filled their veins for the honored task of washing out the stains of slavery?"

Besides, if the Greeks had not claimed and won these rights as they did, the Turks and the Greeks together would have been very likely to have fallen one common prey to another conqueror. Within the mighty empire of Russia the empire of Hellas would have run great risk of losing the very consciousness of her nationality, and would certainly not have regained independence.

Napoleon Bonaparte's expedition into Egypt appeared in the eyes of the Greeks as a war of civilization against savagery, of the Christian against the Moslem. Rhigas called on the victorious French general to plead for the aid of France in the national movement for which Rhigas was laboring. The hope of the Greeks in this direction was not realized. They found that they could count on no help from Western Christendom, so they turned toward Russia.

The Greeks appealed to the West as the descendants of the old Hellenes, in the name of her historic past, and as Christians with the traditions of the Byzantine empire.

The empire of Rome had been absorbed by Hellenism. The Greek language, Greek civilization, the profession of a common Christianity had united the Romans with the Greeks. The imperial Byzantine tradition went on in the Church after the fall of the empire, after the fall of Constantinople. Her calendar of fasts and festivals still celebrates year by year the commemoration of events in Byzantine history. All these things tended to bring the empire home to the Greek revolution, and with that recollection to combine the hope of the resurrection of the Greek empire. The schemes for a restoration of the empire from Charles VIII. to Catharine II. had been incentives to this dream of a new Byzantium. Alongside of this dream the thought of old Hellenism brightened more and more clearly.

In a foregoing chapter it has been shown why the Greeks, with all their love for the memory of the Komnenoi and Palæologoi, hold still more sacred the memory of their ancient heroes. Fifty years before the war of independence they wrote to the Czarina: "Set free the children of the Athenians and Lacedæmonians from the crushing yoke under which they groan, and which, nevertheless, has not been able to destroy the spirit of their nation, where the love of freedom still burns. Our chains have been powerless to stifle that love, for we always had set before our eyes the living memory of our heroic fathers."

The two ideas to restore the Byzantine empire and to reawaken ancient Hellas became intermingled. There was as much of the one as of the other in the minds of those who prepared the national movement in 1821. The poet Rhigas addressed his passionate appeal to every Christian in bondage "to light a fire which should wrap all Turkey, from Bosnia to Arabia."

The Byzantine project was then not so visionary as it now seems. The spirit of nationalism had not been roused in the other races of the Balkan peninsula. They felt that they all were Christians.

The other states might have united under the leadership of Greece to form one Christian state if the revolution had been better organized. If Ypsilanti had possessed the genius of a Washington or of a Napoleon, the great idea of a restored Byzantine empire might perhaps then have been realized. The rising of Wallachia was soon stamped out, and the struggle for independence became limited to Greece alone. Since then the Byzantine idea was more and more abandoned for the Hellenic idea. The war of independence became an exclusively Greek war, and since the formation of the new Greek kingdom the Greek aspirations have become exclusively Hellenic. The centre of Greek thought is in Athens, and in Athens dwells the hope of Greece's future, the hope that Hellenism may again be what it has been.

In the first of the foregoing chapters an historical sketch of the Byzantine empire is given in order to show the most extraordinary misrepresentations which have existed until recently in regard to this history. In the second chapter another historical sketch exposes the erroneous views which have prevailed in regard to the relation of the Greek of to-day to the Greek of the classical period, at least the Greek of the Attic orators. Chapter III. shows what absurd ideas were in vogue in regard to Greek pronunciation. The fourth chapter gives an account of the misery into which the Greek world was thrown during the centuries of Turkish bondage, of the wonderful rising of the Greek people from the lethargy caused by slavery, and of their spiritual and political resurrection. Now we come to the strangest and the most incomprehensible of all the wrongs done to this noble race, the treatment received from the European powers while she was struggling for liberty after long centuries of terrific vicissitudes, under circumstances which presented more difficulties than any other nation had encountered.

Toward the end of the year 1822, the European sovereigns and their ministers were assembled in the council at Verona to consider the Greek question.

In the spring of the preceding year the monarchs, assembled at Laybach, had deliberated already over the news of an insurrectionary Greek movement. Alexander I. and the whole of Europe disowned and condemned the Hellenic war of independence from the very moment it began.

The Greeks in their assembly at Epidauros on January 15th, 1822, proclaimed: "Our war against the Turks is not the outcome of seditions and subversive forces, nor the weapon of party ambition. It is a national war, undertaken with no aim save that of regaining our rights, and preserving our existence and our honor." Their appeals and proclamations remained perfectly futile. The world continued to regard them as subjects in rebellion against their lawful sovereign.

They hastened to send a mission to the Congress of Verona to explain their wishes and plead their cause. The Congress refused, thanks to the influence of Prince Metternich, even to receive the petition. They forbade the Greek representatives to set foot in Verona, and requested the Pope to expel them from Ancona.

It was in the lurid glare of Chios that the powers met at Verona to declare "that the sovereigns had determined to repel the principle of revolution without inquiring in what shape or in what country it made its appearance," and Wellington was the voice of Christian constitutional England on that occasion.

Chios is an island with a population of one hundred thousand Greeks. This island was a kind of an apanage (mastic patch) of the Sultana mother. Chios became the garden of the archipelago. It drew to itself all that was refined, intelligent, and cultivating in Greek society. Schools, colleges, libraries were founded and flourished. The Chiotes took no part in the struggle, but in April, 1822, Moslem fanaticism let loose upon them the hounds of hell. Fire, sword, and the still more deadly passions of fanaticism and lust ravaged the island for three months. Of one hundred thousand inhabitants not five thousand were left alive upon the island; forty thousand of both sexes were sold into slavery, and the harems of Turkey, Asia, and Africa are still (fifteen years after the massacre, when Richard Cobden wrote this, while he visited the stricken island) filled with victims.

Gladstone has characterized it as "that horror, that indescribable enormity, that appalling monument of barbarian cruelty, a scene from which human nature shrinks shuddering away." Such was the massacre of Chios, unparalleled in modern history, a tragedy compared by the British consul, an eye-witness, to the destruction of Jerusalem, which thrilled Europe and America with horror.

After the Congress of Verona war went on, a butchery sanctioned by Christian Europe in the interest of toppling thrones and a balance of power.

"During the last twenty-five years," says Bikelas, "a number of new states have been admitted into the European family of nations, and that sometimes after defeats instead of victories, and sometimes after the populations have merely allowed themselves to be massacred without making any resistance. In view of these facts it is difficult to realize that Hellas, after having fought and triumphed by sea and by land for two years, and thus virtually acquired independence by her army, entirely failed to make the governments of that epoch even listen to what she had to say. Diplomatic Europe was at that time guided by the principles of the Holy Alliance, and these principles were ironically depicted by the Duc de Broglie in one of his speeches: "Every revolution whatever is not only a rebellion against the government which it attacks in particular, but a criminal attempt against civilization in general. Every nation which tries to gain its rights, when its government has refused it the liberty, is a nation of pirates which ought to be outlawed and proscribed by all Europe. Constitutions have no lawful source except in absolutism. Any government which is the child of a revolution is a monster which ought to be killed as soon as possible."

It was against such doctrines as these, as much

as against the army of Turkey, that Hellas had to contend in order to conquer her independence. The powers were exceedingly tender about the sovereign rights of Turkey. They left Hellas to her fate in the conviction that it would not be long before the Sultan would crush her. The little nation had no organization, no resources, no allies, and no protectors; but the energy of despair gave tenfold force to the Greeks to resist the formidable Turkish power.

The Greeks went on fighting, and prospered for two years after the Congress of Verona until the armies and fleets of Egypt came to the aid of Turkey. The Greeks were beaten, still they contested their burnt and blackened fields against the Arabs, and with the continued cry of Ἐλευθερία ἢ θάνατος they appealed to the conscience of Christian Europe.

Then despite their governments the nations began to show sympathy with Hellas. Material help and moral support came from all sides. In Germany, in England, in France, societies were formed for the support of the Greeks. The head-centre of these societies was the banker Eynard in Geneva. Philhellenic volunteers organized, and one of these volunteers was Lord Byron. The first result of this favorable condition was the negotiation of a Greek loan in England.

One time France took the lead in the Philhellenic movement. This nation was entirely free from selfish motives. A philanthropic society for the support of the Greeks was founded in Paris, and this society prepared the way for Philhellenism in all ranks of society, the king's family included. The French press took a most active part; and among many prominent writers in favor of the Greeks was Chateaubriand, who said that the world of learning and the political world were longing to see the re-establishment of the mother of sciences and religion, and to see the altars free again in a Christian country where St. Paul had preached the unknown God. The warmth and the courage with which the Greek cause was taken up in France awoke old sympathies in Switzerland and Germany. Banker Eynard of Geneva, the president of the Philhellenic society, was said to be more Hellenic than Hellas' best citizen. He became the head-centre of the whole Greek movement in Europe.

The first active participation came from Germany. The language of human generosity knew no bounds. Dr. Iptis, Ypsilanti's physician, came to Austria to excite sympathy for the Greeks. In Vienna friends had to aid him to flee quickly to save him from the fate of Rhigas; in Germany he was everywhere enthusiastically received. Among the many noble Germans who worked for the Greek cause were Krug and Thiersch. The German journals gave correct news and explanations about the Greek rising and refuted the Austrian calumniations until the Austrian and German governments interdicted the Philhellenic agitations.

When the news of the massacre of Chios was published in England and Waddington described the terrible distress in Athens, where over twenty thousand poor refugees were starving, contributions were made quietly without ostentation. Erskine, in a letter on the situation in Greece to the Earl of Liverpool, London, 1822, attacked the league between England and the Porte, the fraternity between the king and the Sultan, and characterized this relation as a disgrace to the English nation so long as the ruin of Chios was not atoned for. But only under Canning did *The Quarterly Review* adopt a friendly attitude toward the Greeks, and only then were Philhellenic societies organized. This was the time when the first loan was made to Greece.

Moral encouragement, material aid, political support were needed to help the Greek nation in her struggle; and help came from Occidental Europe. Admiration of the heroic deeds, and sympathy with the sufferings of the little nation showed itself in unselfish exertions. Indeed, the record of this Philhellenic movement fills one of the most beautiful pages in the history of mankind. The ladies of the highest rank in Paris formed special sodalities; organized in different divisions, they made house-to-house collections in the city. In all *salons* it became the custom for the lady of the house to take up a collection for Greece. In the French provinces this new zeal took root and spread. Eynard took charge of the forwarding of provisions; he and his friends sent 24,000 francs in cash, the committee of Paris 60,000 francs, Amsterdam 30,000, and the society in Stuttgart a similar sum. When the sad news of the fall of Missolonghi was made known, when the Bishop of Arta asked help for the wives and children who were sold like cattle, transported to Egypt, never to return—and when Eynard transmitted this appeal to Paris, and from Paris to all parts of the world, all Europe was filled with pity, a pity which confers lasting honors on society of those times. King Lewis of Bavaria had already given from his own money 20,000 florins, and he added 20,000 francs to buy the liberty of Missolonghians sent into slavery, and later on again 20,000 florins of his own money and 26,000 francs contributed by the royal family. He interdicted all festivities in his realm, requesting that the money intended therefor should partly go to the poor of the respective communities and partly to the Greeks. The Philhellenic Union in Munich sent 65,000 francs, similar contributions came from Dresden and Leipsic, where Tiedge and W. Müller kindled the fire; while in Berlin it was the great physician Hufeland and the historian Neander who first made appeals to alleviate the sufferings and to buy the liberty of prisoners sent into slavery. Berlin sent 240,000 francs. In The Hague, in Namur, Bruxelles, Luxemburg, Stockholm, this example was followed. In France the deep indignation caused by the fact that Frenchmen had taken part in the destruction of Missolonghi, and sold cannon to the Turks, gave a sharp impulse to the sense of national honor. In the French chamber Chateaubriand made a motion to punish Frenchmen who aided the Turks; French subjects were forbidden to hire out their ships for the transportation of Greeks into Egyptian slavery; Alexis de Noailles moved that 300,000 francs be given to the French consuls to buy the liberty of Christian slaves, and Constant rose to ask the Minister of War whether among the French officers, who together with the Egyptian hordes had covered their hands with the blood of the Missolonghians, there were any who were still on the rolls of the French army, and whether they still held commissions and still received pay.

All international jealousies disappeared in those days. Eynard expressed his deep indignation when, at the catastrophe of Missolonghi, English politics prevented the besieged Greeks, dying of starvation, from being supplied with food from the Ionian Islands. If he had been governor, instead of Maitland (one of the most detestable, cruel monsters among the enemies of the Greeks), he would have acted differently, even if he were to have died on the scaffold.

In England there were published venomous accusations against the Greeks and their government, in order to defend the English policy, representing that all aid of the people was wasted on unworthy subjects. It is true, some unavoidable mistakes were made by the Greeks in applying the money sent by Philhellenes; sometimes they trusted egoistic people. There were English and even American contractors who enriched themselves by cheating the Greeks, notably two firms in New York, Rowland, and Le Roy Bayard & Co., against whom the United States Government had finally to proceed, in order to recover part of the money paid to them by Greeks for ship contracts.

The leaders of the Parisian Philhellenic unions, however, did not allow themselves to be influenced by the occasional misappropriation of money nor the ill-treatment of Frenchmen in Greece. These leaders were mild in their judgments; they looked with admiration at Greek bravery and Greek perseverance.. They always reported favorably on them, overlooking the evils which, naturally enough, were unavoidable in such a chaos of misery and want of insight and order. The Greeks have southern blood, they are known for their quick impulses. While they formerly displayed pride and sometimes hatred toward foreigners, they were now filled with heartfelt gratitude. They knew that without the intervention or the generosity of the foreigners their country would have succumbed, and they appreciated the more keenly their obligations toward the French because, firstly, they had had to overcome the policy of their government, and secondly, they had succeeded in making all European nations co-operate with them in the work of charity. At the end of the fearful year 1826, the Parisian committee had sent 2,500,000 francs. Even in Vienna the ice melted and contributions came in; and in America there was great activity in behalf of the Greeks, with happy results.

This popular sympathy, this public opinion in favor of Greece, however, became an additional reason for the rabid hostility with which the governments regarded the Hellenic cause. "How is it possible to doubt," wrote Count Bernstorff from Berlin, "that the safety of European society is menaced by the war which threatens Europe, when we see that every revolutionist in every country is making it the object of all his hopes and expectations? . . . It would appear that their aim in wishing to have Greece free is only that they may set free the spirit of evil in all the Christian states of Europe; they hate the Turks only in order to satisfy their hatred of the allied powers, and they call for the intervention of Russia with the treacherous hope of thereby dissolving the union which curbs them, restrains them, and chastises them." The powers never dreamed of doing anything when they heard of the massacre of Chios and of Constantinople, of Cydonia. It was only when Greece, broken down by the struggle, fell a prey to anarchy, when the men of the fleet took to plundering the seas of the archipelagos that Europe found it necessary to put an end to the war, when Prince Metternich wrote that in the near future there might be no more Greeks left to be delivered. When the powers thus were obliged to put an end to the war they wanted to do it without cutting Greece clear of Turkey. In their treaty of July 6th, 1827, each of the powers tried to turn events to its own advantage or to prevent their turning to the advantage of some one else. There was only one point upon which they were all agreed—and this was, to prevent the formation of any Greek state strong enough to be really independent. Emperor Nicholas, in an interview which he held with the Austrian ambassador, assured him that he detested the Greeks, because he regarded them as subjects in rebellion against their lawful sovereign; that he did not wish that they should become free; that they did not deserve freedom, and that if they were to succeed in obtaining it, it would be a very bad example for other countries.

During the whole of the war Austria—the most implacable of her enemies—did everything possible to hinder Greece's regeneration. Prince Metternich, as was remarked by the Duke of Wellington, gave himself up "body and soul" to the Turks as far as regarded Greece. He looked upon the Greeks simply as rebels against their lawful sovereign. The Greeks complained bitterly of the conduct of the Austrian ships, which they represented as being the most effective allies of the Turkish cause. The Austrians transported convoys and munitions of war to the Turkish garrisons and fortresses, and broke through the Greek blockades—acts which were more than a gross violation of neutrality, they amounted to a direct participation in the war on the side of the Turks.

The Hellenes owe much to Byron, Canning, and Gladstone, and the English people, although the English government had not done half as much for the Greeks as has been done in the attempt to fashion an independent Bulgaria.

Among the many enemies of the Greeks who do their nefarious work in the daily papers or other periodicals is a man who signs his articles "W. J. S.," who with venomous malevolence makes plausible misstatements, which go to make up that tissue of splendid mendacity which is deceiving some people who are not familiar with history. This W. J. S. is a Mr. W. J. Stillman who was United States consul in Crete during the years from 1866-68. In 1874 he published his book on the Cretan insurrection of 1866-68. Strange it is that W. J. S., or W. J. Stillman, leads a double life, as Mr. Gennadius has so clearly exposed in a letter from London dated April 1st and published in *The Evening Post*. While his book is fair and correct, his articles of recent date are the contrary. Both Mr. Bikelas and Mr. J. Gennadius, another brilliant Greek scholar and writer, and a historian and philologist well known also in English literature, have answered this Jekyl-Hyde. Since there is so much quoted from Mr. Bikelas it may be well to quote now Mr. Gennadius. When W. J. S. (Hyde), says Gennadius, comes to survey past history, he (Jekyl-Hyde) declares that this contemptible little state of Greece "owes its existence and every foot of ground over which its rule extends" to the great powers. "Not an inch of territory has ever been won by Greek effort." How we lament, continues Gennadius, the fact that Mr. Stillman (Dr. Jekyl) has not also written for us a history of the Greek war of independence. We might then have appealed to him against W. J. S. (Mr. Hyde). For every one, except W. J. S., knows that the Greek war of independence—the most noble and most glorious struggle for liberty which modern history records—had already been waged for seven long and terrible years by a handful of heroes against the then dreaded power of the Ottoman empire before any of the great powers stirred a finger in behalf of Greece, nay, they were all opposed to Greece. The Greek insurgents were branded by the European governments (as related in this chapter), as malefactors and outlaws. Austrian men-of-war, continues Gennadius, did scout duty for the Turkish fleet. The cabinets of Europe championed the diplomacy of the Porte. Lord Ellenborough, a member of the British administration, declared that the Sultan had absolute right to do just as he pleased with his unruly subjects. But the splendid heroism, the fortitude, and the self-reliance of the Greeks aroused at last the public sense of Europe to such a pitch that the governments were compelled to intervene, and the battle of Navarino ensued. Even that was speedily regretted, neutralized, and lamented as an untoward event. Finally the Cretans, who had practically conquered their freedom, were ordered back to the old servitude.

In the first chapter the name of the Klephts is mentioned. Since the newspapers during the recent war translated this word as bandit or brigand, it may be well to state here who these men really were.

The Klephts of old defied their oppressors; they kept the tradition of their nationality vivid, and the love for their freedom burning, until the time arrived when these bands became the chief instrument of their country's liberation. Their life was a wild and lawless one, but there was an element of chivalrous nobility and simple grandeur about them that was admired even by their enemies. The attacks and depredations of the Klephts were directed against the Turks alone, upon whom they retaliated for every wrong inflicted upon their countrymen of the towns and villages. A raya family which had a son in the mountains was far more secure from the exactions and insults of the Turks than one whose submission was complete. The halo of a national glory encircled, therefore, the existence of these men, who were looked upon as the champions of faith and independence. They, on their part, justly considered themselves as a superior caste to the common rayas, who trembled at the sight of the Osmanli. The answer Kolokotronis gave to those who advised him to submit is a characteristic example of the high and independent spirit which animated these men. He said: "The Turks have murdered other Greeks and made slaves of many; but we have lived free from generation to generation. Our king was killed in battle without making peace, his guard has since kept up the fight and some of his castles are still unsubdued. We, the Klephts, are his guard, and Maina and Souli his castles." Thus lived these men, unconquered and unsubdued, until the day when they freed the land of their fathers of the infidel pest, and hailed a new king.

CHAPTER VI.

THE KINGDOM OF GREECE BEFORE THE WAR OF 1897.

THE powers had witnessed the tremendous sacrifices of the heroic little nation, which under the black night of tyranny held out the torch of liberty, of the nation which had fought until her land had been devastated and her race decimated. Finally, after the famous blunder of Navarino, the untoward event as Palmerston called it, they declared Greece an independent state and offered its throne to Prince Leopold of Saxe-Coburg-Gotha.

The object of the war of 1821 was to free the entire Hellenic race from the Ottoman yoke. This was the watchword of Rhigas and the Hetairia, this was what Ypsilanti proclaimed in his declarations, and the voice which was heard amid the sound of the nations rising from the Danube to Tenaron, from Souli to Cydonia, from Athos to the Cretan Ida. The first national assembly proclaimed at Epidauros that this was their object, and it has been to this end that blood has run in every Greek country of Europe and Asia. The great powers of Europe allowed only a small portion of the Hellenic territory and the Hellenic race to recover their independence.

Prince Leopold, who first had accepted the crown, resigned because he could not consent to the mutilation of Greece and to the injustice that Greeks should desert their brethren, who had fought along with them to set their country free; he could not consent that these very Greeks should now be cut off to be sent back into Turkish slavery.

This abdication of Prince Leopold was the formal condemnation of the policy of the powers, especially of English policy. The English government indeed acted throughout as the advocate of Turkey; its aim was to take from Turkey and to give Greece as little as possible.

Prince Leopold had failed to obtain any of the concessions which he regarded as indispensable conditions of stability and progress for the state which he had been called to govern. On February 9th, 1830, he wrote to the Duke of Wellington: "I have considered the protocol of the 3d inst.; it appears that, if its spirit be duly executed, it will affect as follows: 1. It will establish an armistice and *de facto* peace between the contending parties, provided peaceable means suffice to carry this purpose. 2. It will give birth to a Greek state and promise its independence. 3. It will have traced out for this state boundaries, weak from a military, poor from a financial point of view. 4. It will have found a sovereign for the new state." The obstinacy with which freedom was refused to Crete appeared to him especially unjustifiable. "As I see everywhere," he wrote in the same letter, "that it is English policy to separate Candia from Greece, I am afraid that the hidden interest which caused this separation to be determined on will augur no good to the new state. The exclusion of Candia will cripple the new state, morally and physically, will make it weak and poor, expose it to constant danger from Turkey, and create from the beginning innumerable difficulties for him who is to be at the head of the government." The subsequent history of Crete and of Greece has amply justified his sorrowful foresight.

This combination of interestedness and insincerity upon the part of England and the other powers of Europe is all the more repulsive when we examine the history of the Turks and the motives why they are protected and succored by the powers. In the foregoing chapters we have seen that wherever they have set their foot, there they have brought ruin and devastation; the finest lands of the universe have been turned into deserts, and the most intelligent races have degenerated under their sway into nomadic tribes and arrant outlaws. Cities have fallen into dust, and arts and science have fled before this wild herd of savage debauchers. They are the people for whom the powers sacrificed, and sacrifice to-day yet, justice and humanity. Turks have recorded their national life on the pages of history by a big dark blot of blood and infamy, and the names of the powers are to be associated with them as their protectors.

France had recommended to the other powers the emancipation of the island of Crete, but neither the French Government, nor Kapodistria, nor Prince Leopold were able to shake England's opposition to the emancipation of Crete.

The Nemesis for all this English wrong toward Greece has not been waiting long. Thomas Davidson, in a paper entitled "Victorian Greater Britain and its Future" (*Forum*, July, 1897), has depicted it, showing again the truth of the German proverb, *Die Weltgeschichte ist das Weltgericht*. Davidson says:

"While Russia is frankly despotic and opposed to democracy, and Germany is rapidly becoming so, both thus assuming a definite direction and aim, Great Britain is wasting her opportunities and strength in trying to follow two courses at once. She is internally divided against herself. Being more than any other nation dependent upon a state of peace, she has to sacrifice interests of humanity, honor, and authority. She is in a corner where she is compelled to aid her rivals in disgraceful acts against humanity. She has stood by while Turkey has committed atrocities upon her Christian subjects such as would have disgraced the most barbarous nations in the darkest of the dark ages. Nay, she actually has lent her aid in carrying out the policy of Russia and Germany—the two greatest foes of human liberty—in coercing Crete, humiliating and paralyzing Greece, and thereby crushing out all movement toward freedom and democracy in the East. She has become the instrument of dirty work for the despotic nations."

On February 13th, 1833, Prince Otho of Bavaria, who had been proposed by France, was named King of the Hellenes. His father, King Lewis, insisted upon the annexation of Crete, but was no more successful in obtaining it than had been Prince Leopold. Otho was sent to reign over a country of which Thiersch said: An Hellas which did not embrace the Ionian Islands, nor Crete, nor Thessaly, nor Epirus, did not deserve the name, and was incapable of either maintaining her own independence or of educating herself for the destiny to which Providence seemed to be calling her.

Leopold became King of Belgium. He has been called the first of statesman-kings of his day or perhaps of his century. How fortunate for Greece would it have been if this man had become her ruler, a full grown man of thirty, and a trained soldier! Belgium secured under him and his son Leopold II., the present king, sixty-five years of wise and steady rule. Unhappy Greece got King Otho, a princeling of seventeen, absolutely ignorant of kingcraft, utterly incompetent to govern a people new born from a bloody war. It is true, Otho was animated by excellent intentions, a love of justice, and thoroughly devoted to his adopted country; but all these good qualities were not sufficient; it required more to meet the difficulties of the task imposed upon him.

What Leopold was too wise to undertake,

Europe committed to this child Otho, and as we shall see further on, held Greece responsible.

With the establishment of the kingdom in Greece the sovereigns of France, Great Britain, and Russia pledged themselves for a loan of 60,000,000 francs for the new king. The money was to be raised in three series, each of 20,000,000; the first series at once, the others as the new government should be in need of them. The diplomatic representatives of the three powers in Athens had to see to or to supervise the payment of this debt, which was to be in seventy-two half-yearly instalments. The interest was six per cent, which was deducted beforehand. Rothschild, who put the loan in the market, was allowed two per cent commission. Four millions were lost by the rate at which the loan stood in the market; 11,000,000 were at once to be paid to Turkey for an improvement of the Greek frontiers, which arrangement had been made by the diplomatic representatives of the powers on July 21st, 1832. A pitiful increment of territory was thus conditioned on the payment of 11,000,000 to Turkey by the unfortunate country, which the Turkish mercenaries had rendered a desert. Greece was made to pay for this operation out of this first of the vicious loans.

Of the 60,000,000 francs loaned less than one-third found its way into the Greek treasury. The principal of 60,000,000, however, has been paid in the stipulated half-yearly instalments, the last of these in the year 1871. The history of this first loan made to Greece with all its details has been written in a voluminous work by Professor Herman von Sicherer, entitled "Das bayerisch-griechische Anlehen aus den Jahren 1835, 1836, 1837. Ein Rechtsgutachten." München, 1880.

The king was sent with money, with papers representing Greece's debt of 60,000,000 francs, a debt contracted in the name of the country which was virtually a stranger to the whole transaction, and which was bound down by this load in the shape of principal and interest before it was ever ascertained what its revenues were likely to be.

With the king came a numerous body of Bavarian troops, infantry, cavalry, artillery, and engineers, nine thousand in all, flushed with military enthusiasm. The glittering arms of these fine troops and the golden prospects of the high pay secured by the funds which the allied powers had placed at the disposal of the government were in direct contrast with the sight of bands of irregular and lawless Greek soldiers, a half-clad people suffering under the pressure of famine in a country everywhere laid waste, in which far and wide no tree, no cottage could be seen.

Indeed the war had reduced the surviving population to a state of the most complete destitution. All agricultural stock was extirpated; houses, barns, and stables were destroyed; fruit-trees and vineyards rooted up. The destruction of agricultural cattle was so complete that Professor Thiersch proposed to import ten thousand pair of cattle the first and ten thousand the second year. The professor was laughed at, but he was right; Greece had more need of beef than of Bavarians.

The sword, the famine, and disease had reduced the inhabitants of the mainland and of Morea to about one-third of their original number. There has been no war in modern times in which an equal loss of property and life has been sustained by any people, who despite this suffering have remained unsubdued. From 1821 to 1832 Greece had been deprived of every internal revenue. Her commerce was completely annihilated. The commercial navy which had formerly added to the national wealth suddenly became a drain on former savings.

There were no revenues with which to pay and provision the fleet, to purchase stores and ammunition, to pay for repair of vessels. All had to be furnished from the former savings of the proprietors of the ships. The leading families of Hydra acquitted themselves of this duty nobly. Wealthy families have been reduced to want and thrice suicide has been committed to escape starvation. Even with the immense supplies which Greece received from the Philhellenic committees of Europe and America, the revolution seemed not infrequently to be in danger of extinction from the actual starvation of the whole population.

The establishment of new Greece by the powers was an evident mockery. No nation whatsoever could have flourished under the conditions given in this case. The Greeks were exhorted to be free with their chains half-severed, to run in the race with shackles on their feet, to be a model for the very Europe which from the beginning demoralized them. Europe demanded an impossibility of Grecee.

Of the regency which acted during King Otho's minority no one understood a word of Greek. Had this regency consisted of men more experienced in practical affairs, its mem bers would have felt that their foreign troops were too numerous and much too expensive (they cost 20,000,000 francs in two years) for a permanent royal guard. These Bavarian troops received higher pay than the Greek. Bavarian officers were promoted in rank, while Greek officers and Philhellenes were reduced. This was the first cause of the complaints of the Greeks and Philhellenes against what was called the Bavarian system of the army. The men of the regency were incapable of either understanding or appreciating the quick and fiery, but honest and enthusiastic nation. The Greeks, elated by victory, ridiculed the pedantic forms and vain regulations to which the Bavarians endeavored to reduce them, and which were diametrically opposed to their habits, and useless in reality. The Bavarians, instead of humoring, exasperated them by a show of force. The Bavarians insisted, and men who had fought for their country and had endured untold privations for years past, in order to obtain liberty, and who by their heroism had obtained immortal fame, now found themselves dragged into prison and treated with contempt by men who had no title to power but what chance had given them, and who individually were nonentities as compared with Kolokotronis, Grivas, and Phlessas. A wise administration, understanding the people and bearing with their foibles, would have had a golden opportunity to bring on peace between the people and the government. The mistake once made brought on difficulties which could not be overcome in a country demoralized by many centuries of barbarous slavery and completely unsettled by many years of a devastating war.

In describing now the condition, the politics of Greece, I avail myself of a pamphlet which I found in the library of the Historical and Ethnological Museum of Athens. The author was not named; the paper was written in 1870.*

The anonymous author says: "I desire to put forward what I believe to be a true and impartial statement to vindicate the calumniated, to expose abuse which is simply infamous, and to repel accusations which are directed against the Greek people and which are untrue, unmerited, and unscrupulous. . . . Correspondents take a particular pleasure in endeavoring to make out,

---

* Only after this part of the book was in type did I learn that the author of the pamphlet here quoted is J. Gennadius, the same from whom I have quoted already, and who later on became, and continued until recently, Minister Plenipotentiary of Greece to England.

whenever the chance offers, as black a case as possible against the Greek people."

The author also tells that the English newspapers had refused to accept his statement, and that he was obliged to have it published at his own expense, and thus to come forward in an unusual way.

It was the plea of the great powers that the new government required not only armed protection, but political guidance. But the three flags which floated beside the banner of the Greek cross covered also the distinct interests of the several protecting powers which they represented. This protectorate of the three great powers was a systematic interference in the affairs of the country, thus paralyzing the government, debasing it in the eyes of its subjects. Political passions, thanks to the jealousies of the three "protecting" powers, ran high. The unfortunate country had been made the chess-board of European diplomacy and was rent into three great parties, the English, the French, and the Russian, with the respective ambassador at the head of each.

The young King Otho, perplexed in the midst of this state of things, the more so as he was surrounded by many counsellors among whom existed also a diversity of opinion, committed inevitable errors of judgment. To his credit it may be said that he alone assumed the responsibility for all the actions of his government. This brought on him charges of maladministration for which he was only partly guilty.

The powers intrigued to bring this or that party at the direction of affairs; instead of protecting the Greek kingdom, they worked toward the dangers of revolution. Thus in 1830 and 1840 Russia organized the vast conspiracy of the Philorthodox; in 1843 Russia and England combined pushed energetically the event of the 3d of September (demand of a constitution); in 1847 England excited formidable revolts in Eubœa, in Phthiosis, and Archæa. In 1850 the persistent ill-will of the English government showed itself especially in the Pacifico affair. Lord Palmerston sent the British fleet into the Piræus under the pretext of supporting the ridiculous claims of the Jew Pacifico.

Otho had hardly attained his majority when risings took place in Epiros and in Crete. They were crushed one after the other. In 1840, on the outbreak of a struggle between the Sultan and his great vassal in Egypt, Crete, together with Epiros, Thessaly, and Macedonia, then thought that the hour of deliverance had struck. The Crete population rose as one man, and the Cretans made themselves the masters of the whole island, but supported by England the Turks were able to drown the rising in blood. If the Greeks had possessed the necessary preparations, and if Europe had not come to the rescue of the Ottoman dynasty, the Greeks might even have succeeded in overthrowing it.

Since then things have changed. Turkey regained strength; her foreign relations became such that in case of necessity she could count upon the help of some of the European powers. Maurokodatos in a memorandum placed before King Otho in 1848 says: "When we speak of Turkey, we of course know too much to share the delusions of the Westerns, who, for the most part, neither know her nor (it would appear) wish to know her."

After ten years of absolutism, the Greeks, by a bloodless revolution, wrested from King Otho the constitution of 1843. Things went on better but not until the Crimean war.

The hopes of the Hellenes were reawakened with the prospects which this war between Russia and Turks seemed to open. Russian emissaries brought about a rising in the Hellenic provinces of Turkey. Epiros and Thessaly broke into insurrection at the beginning of 1854. Greek volunteers went to the Crimea. At home the prospect of another struggle to complete the work of independence was received with enthusiasm. Armed bands crossed the frontier to join their insurgent fellow-countrymen. The people, the army, and the court all gave themselves up to the most brilliant dreams. Hellas was soon undeceived. The allies, France and England, would not tolerate a diversion in favor of Russia.

France occupied the Piræus from May 26th, 1854, till February 27th, 1857; the Greeks found themselves reduced to absolute powerlessness, and the insurrection in the border provinces was soon crushed by the arms of the Turks. The history of this Greek inactivity in the Russo-Turkish war is still a mystery. At the moment when this war broke out Hellas possessed an army of between 35,000 and 40,000 men. If she had interfered in the struggle, the result would have been a general rising in Turkey and the radical and definitive solution of the Greco-Turkish difficulties. The states of Epiros, Thessaly, and Crete urged the Greeks to interfere. Hellas, knowing the complications which the general collapse of Turkey might produce both in the East and the West, hesitated and finally consented to yield to the wishes of Europe. She consented to contribute her part to realize the wishes of the powers for an immediate pacification and checked the action which had already begun for the realization of what the Hellenes have desired for so many centuries. This she did after having received from Europe a promise that the rights of the Hellenic race should be taken into consideration. The Hellenic government could not leave the inhabitants of the insurgent provinces exposed to all the horrors of a bloody repression by the undisciplined troops employed by the Turks for that purpose; it therefore decided to occupy the provinces provisionally. Diplomacy saw the danger of a fresh conflagration which the armed intervention of Greece was capable of enkindling. The utmost possible amount of pressure was therefore brought to bear upon the government of Athens in order to induce it to withdraw the troops; these recrossed the frontier upon the solemn assurance of the great powers that the national aspirations and interests of the Greeks should be the subject of the deliberations of the approaching congress.

When the Italians, through their revolution from 1859 to 1860, obtained their independence and were soon to obtain their unity through the help of France, the Greeks hoped that Italy would do for Hellas what France had done for Italy. The Hellenic cause had warm friends in Italy. There were negotiations with Garibaldi, but while this new insurrection was being prepared there began to break out those agitations which ended in the dethronement of King Otho.

There were then, and there still are, those who attribute his fall to the action of English agents. England justified the act. "Her Majesty's Government," wrote Earl Russell, "cannot deny that the Greeks have good and sufficient cause for the step they have taken."

The king yielded without resistance to the revolution which overthrew his dynasty, thus giving Hellas a last proof of his love for her by deliberately sparing her the woes of civil war. He left the land of his adoption with words of farewell full of majesty, and good wishes for her happiness which were dictated by a sincere affection. The Hellenes have not forgotten his weaknesses, but they are ever recalling his good qualities. They remember how he loved their country.

At King Otho's departure in 1862 the kingdom was confined within the same narrow limits which it had occupied when he came to the throne. The statesman-king Leopold at that time had been building up a strong state in Belgium.

King George, the new king who took the throne in 1862, brought to Greece on his arrival the news of the annexation of the Heptannesos. The resigning of the protectorate of the Heptannesos was a generous gift from England, and it was all the more appreciated because it was unexpected. It appears that the generosity was the expression of England's satisfaction at having got rid of King Otho. It certainly gratified the wishes of the islanders and it was considered a striking mark of friendship, and this gave rise to the greatest hopes for the future.

Not all the statesmen of England agreed as to the cession. Lord Derby wrote to Lord Malmeiroy on December 22d, 1862: "I think the measure at any time one of very doubtful policy, but the present moment appears to me singularly ill-chosen. It strikes me as the height of folly to make a gratuitous offer of cession, and to throw the islands at the head of a nation in the very throes of revolution, whose finances are bankrupt, whose naval power is insignificant," etc.

The Ionians have not had to regret their reunion with the rest of Hellas, and to Hellas this annexation was a fortunate thing. How much more might be hoped for other Hellenic lands, especially Crete, whose case is so much more crying because the Cretans are under the intolerable administration of the Turks!

The Cretans endeavored to gain for themselves the same good fortune which had fallen upon the Ionians. They defied Turkey for three years—1866, 1867, 1868. With the exception of certain fortresses, the whole island was free. Acts of heroism and sacrifice again challenged the attention of the world. Hellenes of the mainland came to their brethren in the hour of danger to fight at their side, and opened in their own homes a place of refuge for the women and children of the island. Nearly sixty thousand fugitives found protection.

The deliverance of Crete seemed to be accomplished. Russia and France were favorably disposed, but England, supported by Austria, opposed. Diplomacy fought for the enslavement of the Cretans with as much persistence and better success than it had opposed the deliverance of Greece.

The islanders gained by their struggle nothing but a doubtful amelioration of their condition. A sort of a charter was extracted from the Porte in 1868, under the name of the Organic Regulation, which has never been put in force. At the time of the Congress of Berlin they thought once more that they would succeed; they only received another paper, a sort of a mockery, "*to enforce scrupulously the Organic Regulation of* 1868, *with such modifications as might be judged equitable.*"

The history of the Greek question at the Congress of Berlin and the conferences which followed it is very voluminous, since many documents have been published, but it throws no light on the motives which inspired the action or inaction of each government which took part therein.

The Greeks desired from the Berlin Congress the fulfilment of the hopes which they had entertained ever since 1821, namely, the liberation of the entire race, not only of a fraction, since their government was under no delusion as to the many difficulties with which the realization of that wish had to deal. It felt bound to be contented for the time being with the annexation of Crete and of the border provinces, this being all which was at that moment practicable.

On July 5th, 1878, the Congress assigned to Hellas the whole of Thessaly and a large part of Epiros. The island of Crete was not included. This resolution of the Congress was sanctioned by the Conference of Berlin on July 1st, 1880. But all this was given on paper only. Greece was left to sue the Turk, cap in hand, for the provinces given on paper. When Turkey found that she was not confronted by united Europe determined to be obeyed, she refused to submit. Poor Greece, instead of being able to dedicate herself to the work of internal development, was left to put herself in possession. The mobilization of her forces swallowed up the entire sum of the great loan of 1881.

On July 2d, 1881, three years after the signing of the famous protocol of Berlin, Hellas signed the convention by which Turkey ceded to her the flat part of Thessaly and a small strip of Epiros. She signed this convention, but she protested that the faults of the new frontier would soon give rise to new difficulties and dangers. "Europe," in the words of Koumoundouros, "had allowed her own work to be undone for the sake of humoring Turkey; . . . Epiros and Thessaly have the right to be free, a right which Europe has admitted and Hellas accepted; it will seem incredible to them that the European governments should have played with their sufferings, or should have recanted their own doctrines for no object but to please Turkey."

Greece's narrow artificial limits condemn her to be always looking to her frontiers, and the present Hellenic state has been passing for the last fifty years from one crisis into another, which were followed by periods of exhaustion. Hellas had hardly recovered from the struggles and the sacrifices which it cost her to obtain a fraction of the territory which had been added to her by the Congress of Berlin, when the reunion of eastern Roumelia with Bulgaria and the results of this violation of the treaty of Berlin involved her in new difficulties.

Many hold King George responsible for many evils because he could not retain a stable ministry of state. But the political parties, which in their fight with each other caused the many changes, existed before he was called to govern. If he had attempted to suppress them he might perhaps have brought on greater evils. It was his idea to allow the people of Greece to cause their own constitutional education. The chaos of administration which had so long existed—the average duration of the time a prime minister held his office was not calculated by years but by months—seemed to have ceased when Tricupis took charge of affairs for the first time and remained in office for over three years.

It is one of the current remarks of a certain class of writers that Greece, until she can govern what she has, is unfit to be entrusted with a larger area. When we shall come to consider in what condition Greece has been at the end of the war of independence, and how she has developed in spite of the difficulties which the European powers have caused her, we shall unhesitatingly disagree with this view; but we have a more powerful argument against it. The difficulty Greece experienced thus far in governing the area she has—and this is mainly a financial question—is entirely due, as Prince Leopold has so correctly foreseen and as foregoing pages of these lectures show, to the very restricted limits of that area.

The constant strain on her financially is very severe and is never relaxed; the feeling of unrest, the repeated mobilizations to liberate the brethren who are still in Turkish slavery are impediments to her routine work of internal progress.

The finances of Greece have been the subject of much discussion; to enter into details would require a long treatise by itself. A clear statement has been published by Joseph D. Beckmann, in November, 1892. It is contained in a pamphlet, entitled "Les Finances de la Grèce, étude composée sur la bare de documents authentiques." Up to 1880 the Greek foreign debt (nominal—perhaps but half of the money they owed has ever reached the Greek treasury) amounted to 256,000,000 francs. With that year began a series of heavy loans, amounting up to 1892 to a total of 539,448,421 francs, and bringing the total public debt (nominal) up to the stupendous figure of 818,476,339 francs. Of this sum 130,192,159 francs constituted the floating debt.

This constant borrowing of money had a demoralizing effect on the nation; nevertheless with all her borrowing Greece was not utterly reckless. Tricupis had a constant and rational policy. It was to develop the country by means of highways and railways, harbors, lighthouses, and, above all, to re-establish sound money. In

1884 he spent nearly 70,000,000 francs in taking up the forced currency, but unfortunately the very next year Delyannis lost his head in a filibustering fit (into Roumelia), mobilized the forces, and provoked a new blockade by the powers. Of course he brought back the forced currency, which is now larger than ever. M. Beckmann, in summing up his study of Greek finance, says: "Though Greece has borrowed a large amount of money, she has something to show for it. Thessaly, many miles of road, railways, a respectable little army, and a very rapidly developing commerce. Her budgets have been gradually improving and are now in a stable equilibrium.

But since 1893 a new situation has supervened. Then the premium on gold was sixty per cent, as against thirty per cent in 1891; it reached ninety per cent when Beckmann published his pamphlet. The purchase of gold to meet the demands of the foreign debt (in the budget of 1893, 35,468,596 francs) was a disastrous operation, and commerce was paralyzed by the condition of the money market. Then the glut in the current market of the preceding season cut off the only surplus gold revenue of the nation, and the payment of cash in January became inevitable, for no government can weather a panic.

Four years before Delyannis had been dismissed by the king because he had failed to deal successfully with the financial situation. Tricupis came in; he brought forward a broad and statesmanlike project for dealing with the situation. His plans were not approved; he went out after having stood for fifteen years before Europe as the Greek with an honest and rational financial policy. He came in again. More than once he seemed on the very threshold of success, when the political whirlpool would undo it all. His sisyphous rôle seems at last to have worn him out, and returning to power in 1893 he proposed his now famous provisional reduction of thirty per cent on the interest of the gold loans, and a compromise with the foreign creditors. This cost him his European prestige, and his internal programme did the rest. In his long lease of power he had wiped out the Turkish land tithe, provided for a sound currency, and rendered many a noble service to the country.

Vincent Corbett, second secretary of the English legation to Greece, wrote a report on the finances of Greece for the year ending June 15th, 1896, which was submitted on that date, by

Edward H. Egerton, Minister to Greece, to Marquis of Salisbury. After having enumerated the different difficulties of the financial conditions of the country, he says: "But after all, these considerations must not be taken too seriously. In no country in the world are there greater material resources than in Greece, no country offers greater attractions to the student and the traveller, and no country can boast of a more industrious peasantry or a more intelligent and ambitious middle class. The government does well not to grudge expenditures on roads and railways, and when the country is opened up it will be its own fault if Greece does not enter upon a future of prosperity and health."

What has Greece to show for her blanket mortgage? Sixty-five years ago there was not a mile of wagon road, to-day there are more than three thousand miles built, often over mountains. Thirty years ago there were but five miles of rail connecting Athens with her seaport, now there are seven hundred miles of railway in operation, connecting the capital with most of the Peloponnese and opening up a good part of Acarnania and Thessaly, while the Piræus and Larissa Railway traverses northern Greece, thus bringing it in direct communication with Europe. The

Corinth Canal, which Periander dreamed of and Nero began, has been finished. Lake Koraïs has been drained, not only uncovering pre-historic cities, but reclaiming 60,000 acres of rich alluvial soil. The Greek merchant marine consists of 120 steamers and 1,000 sailing-vessels and 3 ironclads. With a sea line seven times as great as France's and twelve times as great as England's, Greece maintains 69 lighthouses and is building as many more. The average in currants and vineyards has increased a hundredfold and more since the declaration of independence.

Greece offers to every Greek child within the kingdom free public instruction from the primary school to the university. There are 2,278 demotic or primary schools, 281 Hellenic or grammar schools, 41 gymnasia, special schools for agriculture, of war, of the navy, a polytechnion, wherein are taught all arts from chiselling a statue to building a steam engine, and a complete university on the German model, with 120 professors and 3,500 students.

Her little army is smaller than our own (24,877 men in 1893) costing only 2,000,000 drachmas a year, her navy only 600,000. Greece alone among European states has abstained from following the progress of military science, her army contenting itself with the rifle of large bore. Ever since the acquisition of the three ironclads, the question of their supplementary armament has been dragging on, but it has not been solved for economical reasons.

The development of the currant trade was one of the first outward signs of the freedom of Greece. In 1820 there were produced four thousand tons, but the Turks persistently destroyed the plants. The production has since steadily increased: 1830, 8,900 tons; 1851, 40,510 tons; 1861, 42,759 tons; 1871, 81,374 tons; 1881, 124,826 tons; 1891, 167,000 tons.

The last-named quantity was worth to Greece 70,000,000 francs in gold.

The olive-trees form the most familiar feature in Greek landscape. Thus it was of old and thus it continued to be till Ibrahim Pasha cut down two-thirds of the trees. No sooner had the Greeks gained independence than they began to plant olives; in 1834 there were 2,300,000 trees, in 1860 370,000 stremmata with olive-trees, in 1887, 1,742,154 stremmata.

A little more knowledge of wine culture, and a great deal more attention to scientific wine-making ought to lead to a very extensive increase in the export of wine, as Greece can certainly produce better wines than Italy, even including Sicily, and not improbably as good wines as any country.

Greece far excels all other countries in her claims on travellers. No country has the same wonderful combination of scenery as Greece. The view from the summit of many Greek mountains is inconceivably beautiful. From Parnassus you can see peak and plain, island and sea to great distances; from Zakynthos to Asia Minor, and from Mount Athos to Crete, are the most beautiful panoramas known to mortals. In no more northern country, moreover, is there the same clear air—an air that seems to act magically on distant objects. But the innermost secret of Greek scenery is the sublime charm of association.

We naturally feel sympathy for the names of places taught and familiarized at school, when we learned what is the most beautiful in the history of mankind, when we heard first the names that pervade all history, all literature, and are the best in arts, in philosophy, and other sciences.

CHAPTER VII.

GREEK AS THE INTERNATIONAL LANGUAGE OF PHYSICIANS AND SCHOLARS IN GENERAL.*

ALL those who attend the international medical congresses notice an unpleasant circumstance, which becomes more and more marked with every succeeding assemblage. It is the inconvenience caused by the want of one language understood by all. There are some members who understand and fluently speak the official languages; they can easily take part in every debate, no matter which official language is used by the speakers. But few such members can be found; the majority of the participants, and among them frequently some who are most prominent in their specialties, understand but one language, and thus lose about two-thirds of everything spoken during the meeting. They are often unable to enter upon the discussion of a question because they cannot understand the subject mentioned; and if they speak on some

---

*Read before the New York Academy of Medicine, March 15th, 1894.

subject, as a rule it is not understood by at least two-thirds of the participants in the congress.

An illustration of the difficulty thus presenting itself on account of the polyglot condition of these medical assemblies is found in a letter written by a prominent German surgeon, dated December 28th, 1892, to the President of the American Surgical Association, concerning the Pan-American Medical Congress.

The languages of the congress were the Spanish, French, Portuguese, and English. The German was excluded, probably because it is nowhere in America recognized as official.

The surgeon says in his letter: "I do not believe that the physicians of Germany will be able to take an active part in the transactions of this Pan-American Congress, unless they are enabled to use the German language in delivering their lectures."

The difficulty in this case was overcome by changing the statutes, by allowing lectures to be delivered in any language, provided that the authors of lectures in other than the official languages transmit to the general secretary a synopsis, of not more than six hundred words, before a certain date in advance of the date of the congress. A further condition was that a manuscript of each lecture of this kind was to be delivered, before or during the session, to the recording secretary of that section before which the essay was to be read. Remarks on articles read could be made in any language, provided the member making such remarks handed them in, before the close of the meeting, written in one of the official languages. I enumerate these details in order to illustrate how complicated the difficulties of a polyglot congress are. Everybody can complete this chapter either from personal experience or by reflection.

One might think the remedy in this dilemma would be the adoption of a universal language, and indeed, this idea has already for a long time occupied the minds of the greatest thinkers, above all, of Leibnitz.. His attempt was based on the supposition that every act of thinking might successfully be reduced to an arithmetical basis, if it were possible to discover symbols for the most simple comprehensions and for the combination, as well, of such symbols, as, for instance, is done in mathematical science. Already in his youth he aimed at this purpose in a well-developed plan, maintained up to an old age, of a "*Characteristica universalis,*" or "*ars signum et lingua philosophica.*" However, this plan was never realized. As far as his idea was correct, it has been carried out by the signs of the mathematical and chemical sciences. A world-language, so far, exists only in the telegraphic marine code.

As the attempts of Leibnitz failed in the seventeenth century, so also did those of the eighteenth century.

During the nineteenth century the means of communication increased in gigantic proportion, international commerce became of far more importance than ever before, and the attempts at creating a world language were resumed. The best known of these is the Volapük of the Rev. Mr. Schleyer, and the partial success obtained for some time by this artificial language proves the existence of a great desire for an international means of communication.

Whatever may have been the object of Volapük, it could never have been the intention of the inventor, nor could it have been expected of him, to make it an international language for scientific purposes.

It was an idea of King Maximilian of Bavaria to transmit to history a reminder of his reign. He instructed the architects of Germany to design a new style to be named after him.

Such a style of Maximilianesque was created. I have seen, in Munich, houses built after this plan. An architect—it was Semper, if I am not mistaken—when asked to take a part in this creation of the so-called Maximilian's style, answered that such a thing could not be made to order, that a style of building is the consequence of the history, the culture, life, and doings of a great period of a people. If such be the case with a style of architecture, how much more must it be the case in regard to language?

The history of this style of Maximilian's is, that it has no history. This short history is also that of the attempts to create a new world language.

While a universal language, sufficient to satisfy the intellectual want of every people and of every time, can be as little imagined as the equality of all mankind, still such a uniformity is possible in a restricted part of human society, viz., in that aristocracy formed by art and science. It is not the masses who need such a universal language, but the men of science.

Since Latin is no longer used as an international scientific language, the want of such a language makes itself more and more felt as science extends. I do not know if any, and what, serious attempts have been made in regard to this desideratum. I read that the American Philosophical Society has proposed that the question of the creation or adoption of an international scientific language should be considered at a congress which was to be held at Paris in connection with the last exhibition. I read further that the Société de Médecine Pratique had taken up the question, and a commission, consisting of representatives of the principal scientific associations in Paris, had been appointed to study the matter. As far as I have learned, these associations set their face absolutely against Volapük.

Just at present there is much agitation in France for reform of instruction and examination in medicine. The Ministry of Instruction propounded quite recently questions in this direction, to be decided upon by the medical faculty of Paris. A commission of five professors and the rector of the faculty have considered these questions, the principal of which was whether the study of the classical languages should be abandoned. The commission in its answer said: The physician is obliged to use a lexicology which is derived from the Greek and the Latin. Although he may, without having been instructed in the classics, in the course of time acquire a superficial knowledge of the expressions, still there will remain in such a case a sentiment of inferiority because he does not know their origin. In the interest of the dignity of the profession, this sentiment should be spared to the future physician. The commission further said it would be absolutely necessary that, in addition to the knowledge of the classical idioms, the knowledge of one of the modern languages should be required, namely, the German. In the present condition of medical science, which derives its elements from all parts of the world, every physician ought to be somewhat of a polyglot.

The rivalry of the nations is against the employment—as an international language—of one of those principally spoken in the civilized world, such as English, French, or German. In addition these languages are insufficient for the expression of new ideas and for the composition of words. Even as it is now, the English, French, and German scholars have one thing in common: they borrow from one and the same language when new words have to be formed for new things. They borrow from the Greek, from that language which has many claims to be preferred to every other in the selection of a universal language for scholars.

Sola virtus in sua potestate est; omnia præter eam subjecta sunt fortunæ dominationi. This sentence of a Latin poet can well be applied to the Greek language. As Virtue, and Virtue only, is her own master, not, as are all other things, subject to the influence of Fortune, so is Greek, and Greek only, of all European languages, her own master.

If we take up a Greek dictionary written for Greeks, we notice that it contains no foreign words. The Greeks love their language as they love their religion. They are jealous to preserve its purity. The use of a foreign word in Greek conversation is as detestable to an educated Greek as is swearing to a well-bred American. English, French, Italian, Spanish cannot be learned satisfactorily without a knowledge of Greek and Latin; and German, an original language, has become so much confused by admixture with foreign words that a knowledge of at least Greek and Latin is indispensable to its understanding.

The fact that Greek is the only living homogeneous language is one of the many reasons why it should be chosen as the future international language of physicians and scholars in general.

In choosing the Greek no mutual rivalry need be taken into consideration. It is the old, old idiom of a small nation and of a small country. The language is rich and is musical, clear and precise, and especially abounding in combinations. It is able to render every modern idea completely, and already it has, in this regard, given life to thousands of words. In thousands of schools, and in every university, it forms a necessary part of instruction. Not only do we use a multitude of Greek words in our daily intercourse, but our entire medical lexicology, also the general nomenclature of the arts and of sciences, is, for the most part, dominated by the Greek language.

The magnificent structures of the ancient Greeks, their equally splendid works of sculpture, have been so little approached by us that nobody, in the whole world, would entertain the possibility of a comparison in our favor when modern achievements are contrasted with the masterpieces of Greek art. The temple of the Olympian Jupiter, the Acropolis of Athens, the Venus of Melos, the Hermes of Praxiteles, are proofs that the Greeks had a much better developed sense of beauty than any other people of a later age.

Greek art is still alive, for it affords the highest examples for our architects and sculptors. Everybody knows this to be a fact.

The Greek language still lives, the same old Greek which is taught in our schools—taught, however, by the eye only. It is spoken by seven million people, and it is more beautiful and noble than any other language, just as Greek art is more beautiful and more noble than any other. There are, however, but few who seem to be be aware of this fact.

Greek has once before now been the world's language. Its use was extended over a larger territory than the Latin. "*Græca leguntur in omnibus fere gentibus, Latina suis finibus,*" says Cicero. "*La langue grecque deviendrait la langue universelle,*" Voltaire wrote. The humanists at the end of the Middle Ages caused its Renaissance.

Let us hope that a second Renaissance and a brilliant period of the study of the Greek language will ensue, the final purpose of which can only be the greatest possible extension of genuine science and culture.

The colleges have sprung from the Latin

schools of the Mediæval Age; they have, on this account, inherited a steady preference for that language. The general use of the Latin on the part of the learned professions has, in the easiest manner, facilitated the learned intercourse of all. This has now, however, altogether changed. The national languages have obtained their natural rights, and should always maintain them, even if a universal language for scholars shall have been adopted. We must concede that it is impossible to reinstate the old relation the Latin has held—when all the lectures on any subject whatever at the universities were delivered in Latin. Neither would such be desirable.

Virchow says, in his inaugural address as rector of the Berlin University: "It was from the beginning a weak side of the humanistic educational institutions to favor the Latin language. It must be conceded that they could not do otherwise. They found the Latin the universal language of church and law. They were all Latin schools. They only continued what had become a general practice in consequence of the habit transmitted for a thousand years. But for this reason they had accepted an element of weakness. For the classical writers of Rome were in their works way behind the Greek authors. Indeed, the best among them are indebted to their Greek antecedents for their education. The school of Athens formed the background of all learned activity. Our own Western civilization has adopted from the Greek literature the really moving thoughts and the facile forms. Homer, Aristotle, and Plato have continued to be, up to our time, the teachers of mankind.

"Since the Greek authors have again been read in the original, the active interest in the Latin language has been reduced. Still, the Latin remained the principal object of information. But it steadily accomplished less. As the use of the language as such became gradually less, rhetoric was omitted, restricting the study more and more to the grammar. Indeed, instruction in grammar gradually so overpowered everything that even the Latin essay became a pium desiderium."

The Latin, as an international and scientific language, loses every day more of its importance. Indeed, it might almost be said that it is kept alive only in purely philological and theological literature. Latin is a dead and restricted language, insufficient for the present time.

The number of Latin scientific terms, with the exception of the vocabulary for law matters, is inferior to the number of words from the Greek. Moreover, we possess only the written Latin language; the language of daily commerce has not been transmitted. The Latin of the Church, of the learned, is an artificial, a forced language. It can easily be understood why, under these circumstances, the instruction in Latin became more and more purely grammatical; but why the Greek, a living language, a language just as living as our own, has been treated alike in our schools, is a question which should be addressed to all the learned world, in order to expose a wrong that has been committed and kept up for centuries.

"Grammatical schooling," says Virchow, "is not that auxiliary means of progressive development which is needed by our youth. It does not cause that desire for learning which is a presupposition of independent further development; but, on the contrary, it is manifest that many scholars, as well as their parents, regard it with hatred."

Professor John Williams White, of Harvard College, says: "High grammar, philological research concerning forms and laws of construction, should be undertaken by no one until he is well on his course, and, it may well be, by the majority of men never at all. The study of the classics is an effective means of mental discipline, but theoretical grammar does not furnish the best field for its exercise."

Study, like almost everything else in our times, and especially in this country, must be done at high pressure; and no time is to be lost, since many things have to be learned. It is true the Boston Latin School does not do what it did forty years ago—teach boys for a whole year the forms, rules, and exceptions of Latin grammar without even a single sentence of illustration; the "Method of Classical Study," by Dr. Taylor, of Andover, in which he asks seventy-six questions upon the first three lines of Xenophon's "Anabasis," and one hundred and twenty-seven upon the first three verses of "Æneid," I suppose is not in use any more; yet radical change of instruction in the classical languages, especially in Greek, is needed, whether we consider either of these languages as an international medium or simply as a means of mental discipline.

The higher aim in language study is to know the language colloquially and idiomatically.

This cannot be attained by means of the grammar. There is great activity on the part of modern linguists toward devising a rational way of imparting a colloquial knowledge of a language. A number of natural methods have sprung up, and have produced new activity in every country. Not alone the modern languages have been taught by such systems, but attempts have been made to teach Latin after such methods. The best, indeed the only successful one, is the Tusculum system of Arcade Mogyorossy, of Philadelphia, Pa., who was born in Hungaria, where up to the time of the Revolution of 1848–49 Latin served as universal language among the cultured people of the many nationalities in the country. Mogyorossy, although born after 1849, was taught his school lessons in geography, history, mathematics, physics, astronomy, all in Latin. He came to this country, where five years ago he commenced to publish a number of books to introduce his method; a little later on he published the most admirable Latin monthly, *Præco Latinus*, which has now reached its fourth year. The Tusculum system surprises us by its simplicity, the main feature being that the language is taught within itself out of its own material.

In order to command a language, it is above all necessary to know how the people speak. The every-day language must be familiar to us. Whoever knows the conversational language of a nation has the key to the understanding of its writings like the people themselves.

The Attic boy needed for reading the Greek poets, the Attic farmer for the theatre or a public meeting, only the knowledge of the Attic conversational language in its most simple form. It enabled them to understand the tragedies of Sophocles and the speeches of Pericles.

It has often been claimed that there are remarkably few words and sentences which suffice for the common man in speaking his native language, and which enable him to understand even that which to him is a new formation. The every-day language must first be known before acquiring the art language.

Macaulay and others recommend, while learning a language, to lay aside the grammar, as the laws of speech will be easily comprehended while reading good authors. It seems to me that whosoever begins the study of a language with the learning of its rules, will never learn the language, unless he abandons the study of the grammar and commences anew.

So long as Greek is taught in the schools according to the present methods, it will be considered as a language too difficult to be learned, and could not be selected for a universal language.

Greek is a living language and must be treated as such. It is difficult to find a proper expression without using strong terms, to characterize the erroneous common opinion that Greek is a dead language!

We frequently meet with people who, having attained a certain degree of education, make this mistake, while as a matter of fact Greek newspapers are continually published and new books treating of various subjects also appear regularly in the Greek language. An uneducated man may be excused for such mistakes, as certainly professional philologists have contributed not a little to the propagation of such views.

Many professors of the classical languages simply pay no attention to the living Greek, without having even the least semblance of any grounds for such disregard; and yet they pronounce the language of the Muses according to the usage of their respective countries, in the English, Dutch, or German manner. The pronunciation, which ought to be alone the rule, is unknown to them, nor do they wish to know it.

Nothing is easier than the proof that the Greek is not a dead language. The daily Greek newspapers published at the present time prove that the Greek language of to-day is still the same Greek of the classical age, showing merely such differences as each living language undergoes in the course of time. Look, for instance, into the Καιροί, published in Athens. Whoever has been instructed merely at school, on beholding for the first time this paper, will be agreeably surprised to find that he is able to understand its contents without any difficulty. A better and more convincing proof can hardly be imagined.

The fact that the Greek language alone has preserved itself almost unchanged through thousands of years in its original beauty is, in my opinion, as a modern Greek writer expresses himself:

"διότι τὸ ὡραῖον εἶναι ὡσὰν λάμψις τοῦ ἡλίου ἐπὶ τῆς γῆς, διότι τὸ ὡραῖον ζῇ αἰωνίως."

The Greek language has been transmitted together with its pronunciation. The majority of the Greek people, kept in bondage since the mediæval age until 1822, were altogether unable either to read or write.

Much has been said garrulously about the degenerated descendants of Pericles, Socrates, and Phidias. Still, these degenerated descendants have the undeniable fortune to speak a language which Pericles, Socrates, and Phidias would have understood. An unbroken chain continues from generation to generation, and back again, from the Greeks of the nineteenth century to those of Pericles, Socrates, and Phidias.

It is a customary assertion that the modern Greek is a barbarous mixture of a good deal of Slavonic, Albanese, Turkish, and Italian, and of a little corrupt Greek. As we have seen, this is just as untrue as the assertion that the Greek is a defunct language. Naturally, such incorrect views are held among the ignorant. However, as I know from experience, such ignorance is found also among the otherwise educated classes who have studied the Greek language while at college. It is remarkable how the very Greek language, from which every other European language has drawn so freely, has been calumniated in such a manner.

Aside from the Greek as published in newspapers and books, which some are pleased to designate as an artificial old Greek in a new Greek garb, the living and really spoken language of both the higher and the lower classes, of the inhabitants of the cities as well as of the peasantry, is by no means a barbarian mixture, but rather a genuine Greek. Everybody acquainted with this language is aware of this fact. I cite as witness thereof: Ernst Curtius, a first-class expert in both forms of the Greek language, who says in his work, "The New Greek and its Meaning with Regard to the Old Greek," that, excepting a few tracts at the border of the territory where Greek is spoken (as, for instance, the Ionian Isles), "even the lowest Greek uses a pure Greek language."

The question of the physical descent of the new Greeks, which cannot be separated from that of the language, is best settled by answering that of the descent of the language. According to late researches, a Slavonic descent of the Greeks can no longer be maintained. Proof can be furnished that not only are the modern Greeks not Slavonic, but also that no trace of a Slavonic influence can be found, with one exception to be mentioned presently.

A colleague, who had studied Greek and was also a college graduate, claimed, while conversing with me, that the modern Greek and Slavonic languages were very much intermingled. A Greek gentleman, a scholar, on hearing this reproach, replied: "I shall be very much obliged to this gentleman if he will mention even one single Slavonic word found in the modern Greek language." The Slavonic is entirely restricted to the designations of habitations, hills, landscapes, waters, and even then it appears only in occasional places and by no means in all Greece.

In spite of a long-continued intercourse, the Albanese have, if possible, left still less traces in the Greek language.

It is somewhat different concerning the Turkish language. The Turkish dominion was for centuries very effective and oppressive; it cannot, therefore, seem strange if words of the official language have permeated the language of the conquered people. We find some Turkish words for Turkish things, as for instance, γιοῦρτι for a certain preparation of milk, πιλάφι for a Turkish preparation of rice, just as beefsteak, the English dish, is called by this name in all countries. In the written language, however, nearly everything of foreign origin has been carefully avoided.

It is true the works of the modern Greek writer are not of so much beauty as the works of the classical period, but the language is not to be blamed for this. The marble of Pentelicon is not at fault when, in later periods, no Venus of Melos, no Hermes of Praxiteles could be formed of it.

The Greek of the schools is looked upon as a dead language; the method of teaching as well as the purpose for which it is taught are of no account for practical life. Those leaving school, except such as choose philology as a profession, forget what they have learned more rapidly than they have learned it, and thus it seems to be of no consequence to the teachers whether the Greek is pronounced in one way or another. A custom handed down for three hundred and sixty-five years is followed, and thus the necessity is removed of imparting to the language the sound of a living, undoubted Greek idiom.

The French, English, and Russian pedagogues think in the same manner as the German philologists, therefore the Greek language is learned in the respective countries according to the modern high German, French, English, and Russian pronunciation, and forgotten again. The fate of the Greek language in the schools seems therefore to be sealed, unless a better mode of instruction is introduced. A language which is spoken by seven million people is forcibly reduced to a defunct language.

A school which is proud of its scientific teachers should teach nothing that has been proved, and also been admitted, to be unscientific and false. Neither should this be done even with a really defunct language. Nor does it ever happen in regard to any dead or living language, except in the case of the Greek. Instruction in the living languages is not given with an invented pronunciation, and even in teaching dead Latin and Hebrew a pronunciation is taught in the schools which is preëminently based upon the living tradition. Latin is taught as it is transmitted through its pronunciation in Italy, and through the pronunciation of the Italian language; Hebrew as it is really spoken by the Portuguese Jews.

Only with the Greek an exception is made by the school, and just in this case the existence of a living Greek language ought to be a reminder to place instruction in close relation to life, so that the scholar might later employ it for practical purposes. The phrase ought to be borne in mind: *Non scholæ, sed vitæ discimus.*

It is certainly very discouraging to the scholar who, having devoted years to the study of the language, finds that, thanks to the college pronunciation, he must pass among the Greeks in their beautiful country like a deaf and dumb person, neither understanding nor understood.

The time has passed long since when a creative activity in Attic philology and archæology was, almost exclusively, evinced in the dust of domestic libraries with fac-simile and picture book. The number of archæologists, especially since Schliemann, who try to enlarge the knowledge of old Greece in the new Greece, is steadily increasing. There are inducements enough, even without the idea of making Greek an international language, to employ the pronunciation of the now living Greeks. No probability exists that the ancient Greeks spoke like the college professors; certain it is, however, that their pronunciation was similar to that of the Greeks of to-day.

The study of the classics, especially the Greek, has been greatly favored in this country during the past decade by the establishment of an American school at Athens. This school was founded in October, 1892, by the American Archæological Institute, and is supported by yearly contributions from eighteen universities in the United States. One result of the establishment of this school has been the gradual diffusion among cultivated people of a more correct notion of the Greek language, and of the appreciation of the fact that it is not a dead, but a living language.

As the humanists, toward the end of the Middle Ages, brought about a revival of Greek learning in the schools, so may it be that a second Renaissance may receive its quickening impulse in America, and that we may be at the beginning of a brilliant period of study of the Greek language, the results of which can but be most favorable to the advancement of true culture among us.

When we consider the absurdity of the school pronunciation of the Greek, we must regret that a clumsy joke, perpetrated upon Erasmus, of Rotterdam—a joke which certainly does not become science on account of its venerable age—is still taken seriously by many.

I said elsewhere: "In order to command a language, it is above all necessary to know how the people speak. The every-day language must be familiar to us."

"Whoever knows the conversational language of a nation has the key to the understanding of its writings like the people themselves."

"The every-day language must first be known before acquiring the art language."

Should we not feel sorry for the student who begins to learn English by studying the poetical works of Chaucer? In what a roundabout way would he finally be enabled to understand the peculiarity of the language of Longfellow; how long would it be before he would be able to derive any sort of enjoyment from this poet's writings, if he were to learn the English language by reading Longfellow's works exclusively, and in learning it were obliged to parse every word?

The color of a language and the kind of style of a literary work, can be fully perceived only by one who is able to judge how far this language differs from commonplace daily conversation. We do not subject good wine to a chemical analysis by means of acids and salts in order to prove its value, neither do we grammatically analyze a poem to enjoy its charm.

In learning a language we notice one thing: in order to advance rapidly we have to read, in the beginning, only such books as are written in an easily comprehensible style, the contents also to be of an entertaining character. If we choose the more difficult, serious, or tedious books, we shall not advance, but rather retrograde. If we begin with children's stories or literature for the common every-day people, we shall be surprised to find how soon we can dispense with the use of a dictionary. We soon guess and learn new words by reading the context. We thus learn to think in the language, and the more we progress the more we enjoy the better, higher, more serious, classical literature.

Professor John Williams White, of Harvard College, in a series of articles published in the *New England Journal of Education*, in 1878, entitled "Latin and Greek at Sight," recommends the instruction in the classical languages after the manner of teaching German and French, *i.e.*, to accustom the pupils to read at sight, without any preceding preparation. He mentions that the pupils learn much more quickly and better to read the German than the Latin languages, although twice as much time is spent in the study of the latter. Concerning Greek, he says: "It is to be reckoned that it is more difficult to learn to read Greek than, for instance, German; but then there is not so much difference between the two languages as to justify the fact that pupils, after studying Greek for years, are not yet able to read without the aid of a dictionary, or through some other means of assistance, while they learn in a much shorter time to read German fluently."

In order to obviate this evil, he recommends, among other means, that the pupils should study no higher Greek or Latin grammar until they are enabled to read these languages with a certain ease, and also have read a good deal. His claims are rather modest. He says: "The study of grammar should be rendered more practical, especially during the first years. The pupil, after having studied both the Greek and Latin languages for three or four years, should be able to read the Greek writings of Xenophon, Lysias, and Herodotus, and the Latin of Cæsar and Cicero, without either previous preparation or the use of a dictionary."

Professor White, in his suggestions regarding reformation of the instruction in Greek, has not gone far enough, because he, like other college professors, ignores modern Greek. The literary Greek of to-day is identical with the Attic dialect in orthography, almost also in form; the syntax is here and there circumscribed and simplified. There is more difference between the Greek of Herodotus and the Greek of Xenophon than there is between the Greek of the latter and the Greek of to-day. There is more difference between the English of Chaucer and the English of to-day than there is between old and new Greek. The living, the Greek as it is spoken and written in Greece to-day, is the one which should be taught in our schools. The Greek as it is taught in general in our schools is simply a skeleton without life. Our college professors should not look upon Greek as a dead language, and above all they should give up pronouncing it in their barbarous, arbitrary manner.

It appears to me that Greek, taught like other living languages, by one or the other modern methods—Meisterschaft's, or any similar system—is not more difficult to learn than French or Spanish, certainly much easier than German.

If we commence with a regular A B C book, a First Reader, Fairy Tales, then read works of the best modern writers like Bikelas, we shall soon get the aim to acquire understanding, and highest pleasure in reading the old Greek classical authors, much better, and without having to undergo the well-known tortures of the present school instruction. If the acquiring of the Greek language is thus made easier, and the classical Greek literature brought more and more within our reach, Kant's saying will become more obvious. "Even during the dark ages great men

GREEK AS INTERNATIONAL LANGUAGE. 255

have existed. During those periods, however, only those could attain greatness who, by nature, had been stamped for it. Now, since instruction has been perfected, men are made great by training."

If the Greek language becomes the property of all scholars of all civilized nations in such manner that it may serve as the medium of intercourse, there is no telling how great the practical advantage will be along with the ideal gain. The introduction of the living Greek language into our schools would be of not less significance than the work of the humanists at the end of the Middle Ages.

As the humanists in their times fought against the obstinate and clumsy form in which the scholastic science was taught, as they fought against the prevailing professional quarrelling, and the cunning and subtilizing in words, just as much is it timely now to agitate for a reform in teaching Greek in our schools. These men were inspired for the grand inheritance left by the ancient classical nations; they recognized in this inheritance one of the most excellent means of improvement of the mind, and an inexhaustible soil of noble sentiment.

The single individual can accomplish very

little to have justice done to a language which our profession uses already so much in its lexicology in preference to any other; to have this language seriously considered when the question of an international language for scholars of all nations is brought up—a language which gives terms to all new inventions and discoveries, and which cannot be replaced by any other; which is already, to a certain extent, an international language.

> Τίς οἶδε, ἴσως ἡμέραν τινα πραγματοποιηθῇ τὸ ὡραῖον δὶ ἡμᾶς ὄνειρον τοῦτο.—Δ. Βικέλας.

The question of adopting the living Greek of to-day as the international language of scholars has become the subject of much discussion. Many American and European journals, even journals printed in Turkey, have entered into the discussion. Professors of philology in German universities and colleges have found it worthy of reply, and have published their views on this subject in scientific philological periodicals—a subject which was warmly discussed in the New York Academy of Medicine on April 21st, 1894, when I read before it a paper bearing on this matter.

On the whole, the responses have been favorable to our cause. The great number and the tone of the commentaries prove that thought on the subject has been aroused, and will continue. Bikelas, the Greek Washington Irving, after having read my article, wrote the words quoted above in regard to the idea of Greek as the universal language for scholars: "Who knows, some day perhaps, this our beautiful dream may become reality."

I have received many congratulatory letters from physicians, from other scholars, from men of prominence and of high official positions, many urging me to continue speaking and writing on the Greek question.

A German philologist, after expressing himself very courteously in praise of the energy which, he says, I have exhibited, is of the opinion that the idea of having Greek as the international language of scholars will not become realized. He refers to my narration of the failure of all attempts to invent a world-language, and also to my illustration of the attempted official invention of the Maximilian style of architecture. He says an international language for scholars can likewise neither be nominated nor invented. Resolutions to this effect might be adopted, but nobody will learn the language, because nobody has time to learn an extra language for the sole purpose of congresses and periodicals. "Dr. Rose," he says further, "is probably not sufficiently aware that the question of pronunciation does not stand now as it stood formerly: Erasmian or Reuchlinian? but rather: When was the pronunciation of the different words transformed into the pronunciation of the Greeks of to-day? This change of pronunciation of the different sounds—as they are written—has taken place at different periods. When?—that is found by the study of inscriptions."

I do not know if researches have been made as to how German, French, and English have been pronounced in different centuries. I cannot determine whether the result of such researches would compensate for the immensity of brain-work employed, but it appears to me that much time and brain-work have been wasted through the fault of Erasmus. If it had not been for him, nobody might have suggested, or might now suggest, any other pronunciation of classical Greek than the pronunciation employed by the Greeks of to-day. Whatever the scientific value of historical studies of pronunciation may be, it concerns in no way the practical study of Greek. Higher philology should be attempted only after the language has been learned practically.

It is quite true that a universal language for scholars cannot be introduced by force or by persuasion, and that nobody has time to learn an extra language for the purpose of congresses and periodicals.

It is conceded, even "im naturwissenschaftlichen Jahrhundert," as the Germans call it, that a regular and solid scholar should know Greek and Latin; it is conceded that the classics are powerful means to elevate, to ennoble our mind, our character. Since Greek is on the school plan already, there is no new language to be learned; only another, a rational method of learning has to be adopted; it has to be learned practically for practical purposes, as well as for ideal. The most perfect, the ideal language will then speak for itself, and will inspire scholars to unite in agitation for its general adoption.

Dr. E. Engel, in his book "Griechische Frühlingstage," gives the following instruction: "How shall we learn the real language of the new Greeks? Turn over the leaves of one of the many grammars and read something about pronunciation, but then throw it, and leave it, aside, and take instead a collection of Greek popular songs and fairy tales. Finally read comedies which really have been played." I myself had followed a similar course when I undertook to learn the living Greek, and I gave some of my correspondents the advice to do likewise. I recommend the reading of children's stories, above all of Bikelas' beautiful Greek translation of "Andersen's Fairy Tales." The most essential, however, is to speak with Greeks and hear Greeks speak among themselves.

Dr. Engel says: "Whoever has learned old Greek will need not much more than to learn some additional few hundred new words. This is rather easy work, since the roots of these words are old Greek." He says further that a foreigner of classical education thus prepared will understand the Greeks in Greece, and the Greeks will understand him, provided he has the right pronunciation.

To this one might say: there exists in reality no new Greek. Many words which deviate from the literary language of the classical period are as old as the words of the same meaning in the classics, although we cannot find them in our school dictionary.

The methods of learning Greek or any language which Dr. Engel, myself, and perhaps many more, have discovered for ourselves instinctively, is really pointed out as being unmistakably the best when we consider certain facts of physiological anatomy and pathology of the brain. From the ways in which the use of the language is lost, or suffers varying degrees and kinds of impairment, we can learn how it best may be acquired. Monographs, above all Kussmaul's philosophical and elaborate work on the disturbance of speech, numerous articles in our medical periodicals, and special chapters in our text-books on nervous diseases, treat on the defects of speech in their relation to neuropathology. The first to apply the recent discoveries in this direction to the methods of learning and teaching languages was Dr. Howel T. Pershing. He has expounded his views in an article entitled "Language and Brain Disease," which appeared in the *Popular Science Monthly* for October, 1892.

I may be permitted to give an abstract of this most valuable paper: All the motions and sensations of the various parts of the body have their centres in the brain. Four centres are especially concerned in the use of language: the auditory centre, by which words are heard; the motor-speech centre, which excites and controls the vocal organs in speaking; the visual centre, by which the written words are seen; and the writing centre, which guides the motions of the hand in writing. The centres are capable of individual development by practice. Certain pathological conditions instruct us in the relative importance of each of these centres in the different ways of using language. The loss occasioned by the destruction of any language centre is an indication of the defect that must result from neglecting to cultivate the same centre by practice. When the auditory centre is aroused by impulses coming from the ears, we have the sensation of sound; when it is aroused by nerve currents, not from the ears but from other parts of the brain, we have only the memory of sound. For a word to be understood, the auditory centre alone is not sufficient. The sound must awaken the memories of other sensations. The nerve currents passing from one centre to another are called association impulses. Prompt and strong associations must be cultivated as a means of securing clear and vivid ideas. The auditory centre is the first language centre to be developed. A child first hears, then understands the sound of a few words, then it imitates the sounds it understands, and soon can use them.

Here we have the coöperation of the motor-speech centre. The two centres work and develop together, but the auditory centre is the more independent and fundamental. If a child becomes deaf, even as late as the tenth or eleventh year, it also becomes mute, unless special educational measures are employed; in adults destruction of the auditory centre interferes sadly with talking, while destruction of the motor-speech centre does not seem to interfere at all with the understanding of speech. When reading is first undertaken, the auditory and motor-speech centres, with their association fibres, are already well developed. The visual centre now begins to work with them. At first it is necessary to read aloud in order to make the association impulses exact and vigorous. In writing, the visual memory may be an aid to correct spelling. Disease cutting off the communication of the visual centres with other centres causes mind-blindness. The patient sees but does not recognize what he sees. If the affection is so slight that he can still recognize ordinary objects, but not written or printed words, he is only word-blind. Although reading in such a case is impossible, writing is not prevented; the patient, however, cannot read what he has just written. Speaking and the understanding of speech are not interfered with at all. Destruction of the motor-speech centre causes a much more extensive interference with the use of language; the motions of the vocal organs being no longer coördinated, an inarticulate jargon, or the senseless repetition of word or phrase, is all that is left of the power of speech. The ability to write is also lost. Reading aloud is, of course, impossible; but it is also a matter of common observation in such cases that the ability to understand print is lost or greatly impaired. This proves that in most persons direct associations between visual words and ideas, if they exist at all, are too weak to be depended upon.

It is the destruction of the auditory centre which causes the most extensive loss of language. In such pathological conditions in which words are heard but not understood, we speak of word-deafness. There are other pathological conditions in which, although the vocal apparatus is in perfect order, the words uttered are mutilated, deformed, and often totally different from the ones intended. We learn here that in talking the most important association impulses do not go directly from the centres for ideas to the motor-speech centre, but to the auditory centre, which, remembering the sounds by fresh impulses, arouses the motor centre to utter them. Writing is still more interfered with, because it depends upon the utterance-memory, which goes astray without the sound-memory.

The auditory centre is essential to the understanding of what is read. In reading, the visual centre cannot, as a rule, call up the ideas, else destruction of the motor-speech centre would not interfere with reading as it does. Nor is the motor-speech centre directly connected with the centre for ideas; if it were, destruction of the auditory centre would not interfere with talking as it does. This leaves only the auditory centre, which is abundantly capable, for the sounds of the words readily awaken ideas before the other language centres begin to work and after they have been destroyed. The auditory centre is the central station through which the other language centres communicate with the centre for ideas. The sound of a word is the word itself. Printed words are only convenient symbols for recalling the sounds. Thinking requires the use of words, not visual words, but the words heard and uttered. It is true deaf-mutes may learn to read and even to speak, and doubtless to use visual words in thinking, but it is with much more than ordinary difficulty. It is a fact of great significance that those deaf-mutes who have once been able to hear, have a great advantage over those deaf from birth, not only in learning to read and speak, but in general mental capacity.

Let us apply the above facts to the method of learning another language than our own. There is the prevailing school and college method to learn the language by force of memory from grammar and dictionary. By this method it is conceded that the ability to converse is not acquired, but it has been generally assumed that by it the pupil could at least learn to read, and perhaps, if diligent, to write to advantage. Yet, even for this purpose alone, the grammatical method must be a failure in so far as it neglects to train the pupil to a quick perception and a ready utterance of the sounds of the language, for we have seen that the auditory and motor-speech centres do an essential part of the work in reading and writing. Even if direct associations from the visual centre may be cultivated, as in the case of deaf-mutes, why, instead of an easy and natural method, choose an unnatural and difficult one that leads to poor results? What are the results of the grammatical instruction? The vast majority of our college graduates neglect to read the ancient authors. They are not able to read them, but only to make a translation. They find no sufficient reward for this slow and irksome process.

A student, having reached the stage of progress in reading and writing our language, visits our country whose language he has been reading. What he hears at first is almost wholly unintelligible, though the same words in print would be familiar. A little later it is not uncommon for him to hear a sentence without comprehending it at all, when suddenly it will flash upon his mind as though he had seen in print what he is hearing and as if he had pronounced it himself, and then he understands readily. The same thing occurs in listening to one's native tongue when the auditory centre has been slightly damaged by disease. When the student becomes familiar with the spoken language through every-day experience, he reads faster, finding a clearness and vigor of meaning before unknown. It is not because his vocabulary is larger, but because it is more efficient. The auditory centre, which formerly, through lack of practice, failed to perform an essential part of the work, is now, at the suggestion of the visual centre, quick to recall each sound, and, reinforced by the utterance-memory, is quick, accurate, and vigorous in reviving each idea. The work of exchange is now done by the true coin of the realm.

Our civilization, as it stands, is thoroughly impregnated with Greek ideas. Our arts, our letters, our morals, our institutions, our religious tendencies even are based upon Greek culture, inspired by Greek perfection, and renovated with Greek refinement. The study of Greek is not, as it has been heretofore, a mere linguistic discipline, or a purely scholarly attainment, but it means a practical study of the sources and origins of our modern civilization. It affords to the modern mind a better comprehension of the nature and character of our own elements of culture. For this purpose the methods and systems of teaching and learning Greek must be remodelled. Grammatical chicane has to be reduced to a more human minimum; a closer attention to the spirit must be advanced to a really humanistic maximum.

Greek, the most beautiful of languages, will live
ΤΟ ΩΡΑΙΟΝ ΖΗ ΑΙΩΝΙΩΣ!

EPILOGUE.

It is a most peculiar habit of tourists who have been a few days in Athens to write childish articles for their home journals about Greece and the Greeks. I recollect such a paper which appeared in one of our first-class illustrated magazines. The author, a reverend gentleman, had been staying in Athens two days in all. He was addressed as Kurie, and people said kalimerra instead of good-day, and this was all he wrote about the Greek language. Unfortunately these tourists, not understanding the language of the country, are ill-humored and write with malevolence. Their readers at home believe everything, and the most absurd ideas are spread.

Perhaps nothing is more amusing than the involuntary drollery of the man in the shabby fulldress suit in a dime museum. "Here, ladies and gentlemen, you see two busts: this is Cæsar's and the other Pompey's. They are very much alike, especially Cæsar." This is about the style in which the essays on modern Greek history and the modern Greek language are treated in the popular guide books, Murray and Baedecker.

Here is a quotation from Murray's "Handbook for Travellers in Greece," edition of 1896: "The claim of the modern Greeks to true Hellenic descent is a question which admits of considerable doubt and not very profitable discussion. A large proportion of the slaves employed in agriculture during the most flourishing periods of the state were of foreign origin, as we know from the enormous extent of the slave trade. We know also that under the domination of the Romans the higher classes of Greece either died out or lost their nationality by adopting the names and assuming the manners of Roman citizens. It seems therefore probable that pure Hellenic blood began to be greatly adulterated about the time when the ancient dialects fell in disuse." Murray and Baedecker are very much alike.

Baedecker is not less ignorant. He writes: "When a (Greek) priest is made a bishop he must renounce his wife and children, the former frequently entering a nunnery."

This ignoramus Baedecker is quoted, and so

are other ignoramuses who have written about the Greeks, and it is quite annoying to meet people who dispute with you on the strength of Baedecker-Murray authority.

But there are more dangerous people than Baedecker and Murray and the every-day tourist who write about Greece. It is that class to which the professor belongs whose letter is quoted in the chapter on pronunciation. He says: "I have a less high view of the modern Greeks and their language than I had before my recent residence in Athens of eight months. There is absolutely no modern literature worthy of the name." This professor is indeed a man of profound learning, a great Greek scholar, who has written important works on the Greek language; but he is like some other old gentlemen—in the medical profession, for instance.

Our learned professor in the chapter on pronunciation says: "I have a less high view of the modern Greeks."

Athens possesses monuments of art superior to any others to be found anywhere in the whole world. The monuments in Athens date from the most brilliant epoch of the classical period. Every one has heard of the incomparably wonderful climate and magnificent scenery of Athens and its surroundings. I cannot say which of the three impressed me the most favorably: the wonders of art, those of nature, or the thousand good qualities I have seen in the Greeks themselves. The Greeks, notwithstanding their faults—no nation is free from faults—notwithstanding their mistake in going to war altogether unprepared against a foe well prepared, well supported, and thrice as numerous, the Greeks not only have been, but never have ceased to be to this very moment, the noblest race.

There exists no alcoholism in Greece. Even the bitter enemies of Greece, the tourists, who are fault-finding all the time, in their publications generally mention that they never saw drunken people in Greece. The Greeks live plainly, moderately, and much more according to the laws of nature than the people in Europe or elsewhere in the civilized world. Obesity even is extremely rare. There are fewer crimes committed in Greece than in any other state of Europe. The only crimes which are comparatively frequent are those of violence. Southern blood, easily excitable, although by no means ill-tempered — a little dispute about a trifle, words are exchanged, the dispute becomes hot, the blood boils; everybody, at least of the country people, constantly carries arms; the knife or the pistol is drawn—there is a victim. Thieving is extremely rare. Dishonesty among the Greek post-office employees, for instance, is almost unknown. Money is exposed in glass cases in large amounts on the sidewalks of Athens by the money-changers, sometimes almost with as much confidence as the newspapers on a newstand in New York. But we have some illustration right in New York. Here these many years have been and are living between two and three thousand Greeks—mostly young—of the poorest class. I am sure none of them has ever been accused of stealing; at least I never heard of such a case. It is true the police, after having made them pay a license for peddling fruit, continually arrest these innocent people under all sorts of pretexts, because they sell fruit.

From official statistics we learn that in the year 1885, when Greece had a little over two millions of inhabitants, there were in the whole kingdom 1,503 blind, 1,084 deaf, and 1,088 insane. This small number of insane, especially, is attributable to the absence of alcoholism. I studied the statistics of all the lunatic asylums in

Greece, and found that there were years in which not a single case was recorded in which alcoholism figured as a causal factor.

From official statistics we learn the following most interesting facts: Among 5,000 deaths at all ages, there is 1 occurring at the age of 100 years or more. One in 3,020 inhabitants attains 85 to 90 years (in France 1 in 4,354); 1 in 5,918, 90 to 95 years (in France 1 in 20,000, in Saxony 1 in 11,000); 1 in 11,988, 95 to 100 years (in France 1 in 83,145); 1 in 16,678, 100 or more years (in France 1 in 352,947).

No country in all Europe is less afflicted with syphilis than Greece. The reasons for this remarkable fact are the following:

1. The majority of the population—namely, 55.27 per cent.—are peasants.

2. Houses of prostitution, except in some but by no means in all cities, do not exist. This is the more honorable to the Greeks of to-day when one recalls the ancient cult of Aphrodite Pandemos. Even Athens was without a brothel until the French introduced their morals, or lack of morals, during the blockade of the Piræus at the time of the Crimean war (1854–57).

3. The restricted communication between many districts with large cities or foreign lands.

4. The strict morals of the majority of the population. All witnesses agree that chastity is law in Greece. The bitter enemies of this unfortunate country cannot deny that Greek women are virtuous women; that women are nowhere more highly respected.

Our professor was eight months in Athens. He must have seen all the noble edifices, the public institutions of science, art, and charity, founded and provided for by Greek patriots, which adorn Athens. I ask him, Is there any city in the world which can rival Athens in works of philanthropy and patriotism?

Our professor of the chapter on pronunciation says further: "There is absolutely no modern literature worthy of the name."

In Athens the following learned societies exist: Parnassos Literary Society, founded 1865; Byron Society, 1868; Society for the Propagation of Hellenic Literature, 1869; Society of the Friends of Education, 1836; Historical and Ethnological Society, 1883; The Physical Science Society, 1887; Athens Scientific Society; Teachers' Society, 1873; Orient, or Asia Minor Society; Academy, 1859.

Has our professor in the chapter on pronunciation not seen the transactions of these societies?

They can be found in the libraries of Athens, and they alone form a literature worthy the name; but, above all, the professor must know the publications of the Archæological Society! May I ask, are not the books of Papadimitrakopoulos, of Hatzdakis, of Arguriados, for instance, worthy of our highest admiration? Do they not belong to the best of any literature of our time?

The following letter, which I wrote in Athens for publication in the New York *Medical Journal*, however, gives an idea of a work of a monumental grandeur belonging to the noblest of the literature of any country in the world. Is there any literary production in any country at the present time which is superior to this?

ATHENS, *August 16th, 1897.*

To the Editor of the New York Medical Journal:

SIR: One of the noblest buildings of modern times is the Academy of Athens. As is well known, it was built at an expense of five million drachmas, the gift of a rich Greek, Simon G. Sinas. Its features in general, its statues, the gilding, and the colors give an idea of the splendor of classical architecture. All this has been well described and depicted.

However much we may admire this structure

and its beauties, we shall find in one of its vast halls a treasure which is of much greater value still, of a value for science, the praise of which cannot possibly be exaggerated.

It is a collection of skulls and skeletons found in Greece, dating from all periods—the prehistoric, that is, the period of Mykenæ, the archaic, the classical, the Roman, and the Christian—and in order to make comparisons with these ancient skulls there are also skulls of our times from different sections of the country.

The founder and conservator of this collection, which is more important than any collection in any other museum in the world, is Dr. Klon Stephanos, the author of a scientific work entitled "La Grèce au point de vue naturel, ethnologique, anthropologique, démographique et médical" (Paris, 1884).

Each and every one of these skulls and other parts of the skeleton have come to light through the official excavations of the Greek government and the Archæological Society, under the strictest control of men of science who hold themselves responsible to the government and to the world of science. Many of the skulls were taken by Dr. Klon Stephanos himself at the moment of their excavation. The skulls and skeletons are identified as to their origin, that is, the locality where they were found, the surroundings, the grave, the arms, the pottery, the tools, the ornaments—in fact, all that would aid in giving information, nay, conclusive evidence, as to the period to which the skulls or the skeletons belonged.

Here are—an important part of the collection—forty skulls of the prehistoric, of the Mykenæ period—that is, about the fifteenth century before Christ. Let us see what this number of skulls of this early period signifies. Nine years ago—that is, before this collection was begun—there was not a single Greek skull of this period known to science. Thus the question in regard to the two principal peoples of the most ancient Greece—the Pelasges and the Greeks proper—the question of their being brachycephalous or dolichocephalous, and in what proportion the one or the other form predominated, could by no means be decided. Now, by means of this rich material which presents itself here, it may be said positively and surely: Some of the prehistoric Greeks were mesaticephalous; others were dolichocephalous.

Until the year 1884 there were, in the different collections of Europe, about ninety ancient skulls known, of which twenty-nine belonged to

Attica (Nicolucci, Virchow, Broesike, *et al.*), thirty-eight to Asia Minor (twenty-two to Troy [Virchow] and sixteen to Ionia [Zaborowsky]), four to the Greek islands (Quatrefages), and nineteen to southern Italy and Sicily (Nicolucci *et al.*). This shows that there were only thirty-three skulls from Greece, and that from most parts of Greece not a single ancient skull was known to science. There was the impossibility of obtaining reliable results in regard to the most important part of Hellenic ethnography, the impossibility of a comparison of the ancient type with all the later types of Greece.

There are in the collection some skeletons from the oldest Iron Age of Greece, the twelfth to the thirteenth century before Christ, found at Eleusis. The objects of art found with these skeletons show the geometric instead of the naturalistic style, the latter being the style of Mykenæ. Of the Iron Age, the museum possesses a number of skeletons of very small children which had been preserved in vases in the necropolis of Ereusis. At this period the mesaticephalous and the brachycephalous types begin to make their appearance; the mesaticephalous type is the predominating one, but the brachycephalous type is frequent.

The number of skulls in the Museum of the University of Athens, from this epoch to the classical period, is very large, also the number of those from the Roman and from the Christian periods. Among the ancient skulls there are series from Eretria, Corinth, and Bœotia (Thespia, Chorsia, and Tanagra). Of the more recent periods, there are series of skulls from Thessaly, Naxos, Amorgos, Attica, Ægina, and Megara.

Dr. Stephanos takes the measurements according to the adopted international method, but besides he records according to his own method, which gives the best results. As much as possible descriptive terms are avoided; the measurements alone, as a rule, are presented to demonstrate the characteristics. These measurements, as they are written down according to both methods for each skull, show quite an extensive amount of work.

While speaking of measurements, I will state here that Dr. Stephanos has measured more than ten thousand heads of Greek recruits. The results of these measurements are demonstrated on a cephalometric map. On this map the administrative divisions are ignored, since they are often completely neutralized by the result of anthropological researches. Thus, for instance, villages are found far apart, which, according to anthropological resemblances, belong together. By lines of different colors the frequency of the different types — hyperbrachycephalic, brachycephalic, mesaticephalic, and dolichocephalic — is demonstrated in a clear manner, and each conglomeration of specimens of the one or the other of these types can be seen at a glance.

The distribution of the frequency of the different colors of eyes and hair is marked on a special map by lines of different color. This latter map is the first of its kind to demonstrate the frequency of these characteristics for each special type.

Dr. Stephanos has improved craniometric methods by demonstrating certain characteristics by means of measurements, and has in this manner given the value of these characteristics in exact mathematical form; he has also complemented the "seriation" method by means of which we are enabled to determine and to distinguish, in all cases in which different types come under consideration, that part which belongs to the one or the other of the different types, and which are the oscillations and the maxima of frequency of each cephalometric character in each series.

But not only has he improved the different craniometric methods, but he has devoted himself *on a very large scale* to the study so as to give all sorts of elements which can be brought in to aid more or less closely the study of anthropology. In order to carry out this plan, thousands of archives, documents, deeds, ecclesiastical, fiscal, and family papers, especially papers of the Middle Ages, papers never before published, had to be studied, and personal inquiries had to be made in all parts, or among the inhabitants of all parts, of Greece. The results of these researches, comprising every locality of Greece, myriads of names of places, of mountains, of rivers, of families, of words in all the different dialects for things pertaining to agricultural, pastoral, and domestic life, of words from natural history, names for animals and plants, the geographical domain of each phonetic phenomenon of the Greek dialects, are collected in voluminous manuscripts which I have had the pleasure, the delight, to examine.

There is, first, one volume treating of the relation of all facts pertaining to invasions, captures, the captives taken, the transportation of these captives, massacres, and depopulation.

The collection of family names presented in

another manuscript has proved to be of great importance, as one example will demonstrate: In parts where there was a great immigration, as in the island of Zante at the end of the fifteenth century, we find hundreds of family names taken from the files of death certificates. We find these names from the time mentioned down to the present time, and can determine the place whence the individuals came and where they settled with a most surprising exactness and certainty.

There is a map adorning the wall of the Anthropological Museum the like of which has never been executed before in any country. It is a map of Greece during the Middle Ages, with the names of all the villages, places, mountains, rivers, etc., as they were found by the extensive researches in history, in chronicles, in archives, in documents, and in papers that I have mentioned.

One volume belonging to Dr. Stephanos' great work of studying the anthropology of his country in a more satisfactory manner and more thoroughly than was ever done anywhere before, gives the provincialisms, the dialects, and phonological characters of all the words for things, as already mentioned, relating to agricultural, pastoral, and domestic life, the terms of natural history in the people's language, for instance, of the fauna and flora of Greece in all the different parts of the country, and also the description of ceremonies, especially of weddings, in their variety and peculiarity to locality.

The following copy, which I was allowed to make, will serve to illustrate this part of the work; it will also illustrate some of the wonderful poetical beauties of the Greek dialects and the richness of the language:

Ἶρις, *rainbow.*
δοξάρι, *arch,* Syra, Kymi (Eubœa), Cephalonia, Chimarra (Epirus), Eurytania, etc.
δόξα, *glory* (only an abbreviation of a word, not exactly meaning glory), Mykonos, Andros, Kythnos, Karystos, Levadia, Anachona (Bœotia), Doride, Redestos (Thrace).
Θεοδόξαρο, *arch of God,* Nauplia, Lamia.
τῆς γρηᾶς τὸ δαξάρι, *the arch of the old woman,* Leucade (Santa Maura).
δοξάρι τῆς καλόγρηας, *arch of the nun,* Ithaca.
Κεραζώνη, ἡ, *belt of our lady,* Naxia.
κεραζοῦ, Paros, Kythnos. ⎫
κερατζοῦ, Siphnos.   ⎬ The meaning of these words cannot be traced.
κεραζούλα, Sikinos.   ⎪
νεραντζούλα, Thera, Milos, Amorgos ⎭
(ἀνεραζούλα?).

Ἁγία Ἑλένη, Chios, Mitylini (perhaps first Ἁγίας Ἑλένης ζώνη, *belt of St. Helen*).

Κερασελένη, Kos. } Constructions
χερασολένη, Lemnos. } of which no
χερασολέ, Ikaria. } translation can
χουραλησά, Libision (Asia Minor). } be given.

Παναγιᾶς τὸ ζωνάρι, *belt of the Blessed Virgin*, Leukadia.

χαλογρηᾶς το ζωνάρι, *belt of the nun*, Sparta, Messina, Argolide.

χαλόγρηας, Elide.

χαλογρές, Gortynia.

'Αγία ζώνη, *the holy belt*, Syra.

Καμάρα, Megata, Keos, Andros, Kypros.

Λάδι χαὶ χρασί, oil and wine (because the prophecy is: If the rainbow has much of the green color there will be a rich harvest of olives, and if there is much red there will be a good wine year), Monemuasia.

'Ανεμοδόχυς, Mykonos, Tinos.

Μαροῦλι (χαμμαροῦλι?), Magne.

χαπιράνι, Sphakia (Crete).

Dr. Stephanos is preparing a bibliography for his own use and also to aid every student of the subject, giving the titles of all books, pamphlets, articles in periodicals, and manuscripts which treat of the anthropology of Greece or may serve for its study.

The books, pamphlets, prints of all kinds, and manuscripts which form the library of the Museum of Anthropology of the University of Athens, it goes without saying, make the most complete collection of its kind. The nucleus of this library was the gift of the celebrated man of science, Alexander Paspatis, and his widow has given a considerable sum for the completion of this library.

If we take a glance over the whole, the great collection and the great work connected with it which present themselves to the scholar, we may well envy the University of Athens, and Greece in general, which are so fortunate as to possess them. Here is a rich material for the study of anthropology, and a master is here to make use of it as nobody ever before has been able to do. It is especially noteworthy that one single man is working on a scale of such immense proportions.

The Greeks incurred the displeasure of the European governments by their revival of the Olympian games in 1896. The eyes of the world were directed toward the Greeks, and it appeared very probable that many of the artificially kept up prejudices against them would vanish. This, however, as we can understand after having read history, did not harmonize with the politics of the English, the Russian, and the German governments. With the commencement of the Cretan difficulties the press of Europe, foremost that of Germany, was directed to

EPILOGUE.

influence public opinion against the Greeks. It is painful to say there was nothing too base, nothing too absurd in calumniation, but the public accepted it. The journals refused everything that was offered to correct misrepresentations. Most remarkable was the conduct of the German press of New York; here the German *Wahrheitsliebe* was suspended, and *Freiheitsliebe* was not accorded to the poor Cretans suffering under cruel Turkish yoke. The pleasure at the defeat of the Greek army was great; no German seemed to remember anything about the history of the battles of Jena and Auerstaedt, and all that preceded and all that followed. Let us hope that the Greeks may learn from history how the soldiers of 1806—that is, the soldiers from Jena and Auerstaedt—became the soldiers of 1813, the soldiers of Leipsic.

In the Historical and Ethnological Museum of Athens there is a glass case, surrounded by Turkish flags. In this case there are, as the following inscription tells:

ὁβίδες καὶ θραύσματα ὁβίδων καὶ βυλίδες ἐκ τῶν ῥιφθεισῶν ἐκ τοῦ κόλπου τῶν Χανίων παρὰ τοῦ ἠναμένου στόλου τῶν ἓξ Μεγάλων Δυνάμεων κατὰ τῶυ ἐν Προφήτῃ Ἠλίᾳ τοῦ Ἀκρωτηρίου ἐστρατοπεδευμένων 700 Χριστιανῶν Κρητῶν τὴν 9 ην Φεβρουαρίου, 1897, ὥρα 4½ μ.μ.

(Shells and fragments of shells and balls which have been thrown from the Gulf of Canea by the united fleet of the six great powers into Prophiti Ilia of Acrotisi against the 700 Christian Cretans encamped there on the 9th of February, 1897, at 4:30 P.M.)

These projectiles tell of the greatest shame, not only of our century, but of the history of mankind.

It was my good fortune while in Athens to see Professor Hatzidakis, whom I have quoted in the first chapter of this book. He is a Cretan. When the revolution broke out, he left his place at the university and fought for his country with the other insurgents. He told me: "In Crete mourning, poverty, and famine reign. There is no money. People are sadly in need of clothing, and they have no bread." Hatzidakis was with his people. One day they baked bread. This became known, and children in masses came asking for a piece of bread. There was none with a whole garment.

Early in September last I left the Piræus to return home to America. It was two o'clock in the morning when we were passing the isle of Crete. We saw the men-of-war of the six powers; they had illuminated; on board there were music and dancing and fireworks. The brave men who had fired from a safe distance upon the Cretan Christians were celebrating the anniversary of the Sultan's ascension to the throne.

While in Athens Mr. Bikelas invited me, together with my little daughter, to dinner. He listened with great interest to all I had to say about Hellenism in America. "How unfortunate," he said, "that America is so far from us."

In the house of a lady of distinction, where I had been honored with an invitation, I met some refugees from Thessaly—ladies and gentlemen. We spoke of America, and each and every one expressed himself in the very words of Mr. Bikelas.

When you come to Athens, the doors, the arms, the hearts of the people are wide open to you, because you are an American.

LIST OF SUBSCRIBERS.

The author begs to express his sincerest gratitude for being permitted to publish the list of subscribers, which includes the names of many reverend and illustrious men. The object of the publication was expressed in the circular, namely, to identify and draw nearer together the Philhellenes of America. It may serve useful ends to have this list as complete as possible, and therefore all Philhellenes are asked to send in their names for publication in a later edition of the book.

No. of copies.

3 Miss Fanny S. Adam, 13 E. 40th St., New York.
1 Rev. M. W. Adams, Dean Atlanta University, Atlanta, Ga.
2 Mr. A. M. Agelasto, Norfolk, Va.
5 Hon. Eben Alexander, former United States Minister to Greece, Professor of Greek, North Carolina University, Chapel Hill, N. C.
1 Mr. E. Alexander, 41 Fulton St., Boston, Mass.
1 Dr. Rudolf Allert, 502 E. 58th St., New York.
1 Mr. B. G. Amend, 205 Third Ave., New York.
1 Mr. C. A. L. Amend, 205 Third Ave., New York.
2 Mr. Robert F. Amend, 205 Third Ave., New York.
1 Louis F. Anderson, Professor of Greek, Whitman College, Walla Walla, Wash.
1 S. J. Ansley, Professor of Greek and Latin, Howard College, East Lake, Ala.
1 Rev. Archimandrit Chrysanthos Antoniadis, Ph.D., Athens, Greece.
1 Mr. B. Antoniou, Athens, Greece.
1 John Argyriadis, Professor of Philology, Theological Seminary, Athens, Greece.
1 Mrs. F. Bagoe, 423 Fourth Ave., New York.

No. of copies.

- 1 Mrs. Xenophon Baltazzi, 16 E. 40th St., New York.
- 1 Mr. T. S. Baltazzi, Schulenburg, Texas.
- 1 Hon. S. J. Barrows, House of Representatives, Washington, D. C.
- 1 Mr. S. Bazanos, 558 Broad St., Augusta, Ga.
- 1 Lukas S. Bellos, M.D., Athens, Greece.
- 1 Mr. Peter M. Biegen, 558 Mott Ave., New York.
- 1 Mrs. Mary L. Biegen, 1035 E. 156th St., New York.
- 2 Mr. D. Bikelas, Athens, Greece.
- 2 Mr. Francis Blake, Keewaydin, Weston, Mass., Auburndale P. O.
- 1 Mr. James A. Blanchard, Tribune Building, New York.
- 1 Mr. Andrew Blaurock, 604 E. 17th St., New York.
- 10 Hon. D. N. Botassi, Consul General of Greece, New York.
- 1 Mr. John Botassi, Athens, Greece.
- 2 Mr. John L. Brower, 156 and 158 Broadway, New York.
- 1 Prof. George S. Brown, Antioch College, Yellow Springs, Ohio.
- 1 Dillon Brown, M.D., 40 E. 57th St., New York.
- 1 Mrs. Louise Buchtel, 153 W. 23d St., New York.
- 1 Rev. Henry A. Buttz, Dean Theological Seminary, Madison, N. J.
- 1 Arch. M. Campbell, M.D., 36 First Ave., Mt. Vernon, N. Y.
- 1 Mr. Demetrius Carra, 33 S. William St., New York.
- 1 Thomas Carter, Professor of Greek and Latin, Centenary College, Jackson, La.
- 1 Joseph Collins, M.D., Professor Post-Graduate Medical School, New York.
- 1 Mr. F. O. Collins, 131 Third Ave., New York.
- 1 Miss Phroso Colocotronis, Athens, Greece.
- 1 Cooper Union, New York.
- 1 Rev. N. E. Cornetet, Professor of Latin and Greek, Avalon College, Trenton, Mo.
- 1 Most Rev. M. A. Corrigan, Archbishop of New York.
- 1 C. Everett Conant, Professor of Greek and Latin, Lincoln University, Lincoln, Ill.
- 1 Prof. J. M. Cox, Philander Smith College, Little Rock, Ark.

LIST OF SUBSCRIBERS.

No. of copies.
- 1 J. K. Crook, M.D., 36 E. 29th St., New York.
- 1 Andrew F. Currier, M.D., 120 E. 34th St., New York.
- 1 M. G. Dadirrian, M.D., 73 Lexington Ave., New York.
- 1 Dr. J. E. David, 70 Liberty St., Asheville, N. C.
- 1 Mr. J. W. Davis, Public School 81, Bedford Park, New York.
- 1 Mr. M. Diepenbrock, 50 E. 58th St., New York.
- 1 Mr. Angelo Dotorato, 192 E. 125th St., New York.
- 1 Mr. Nicholas Dotorato, 192 E. 125th St., New York.
- 1 T. J. Downing, M.D., New London, Mo.
- 1 Mortimer Lamson Earle, Professor Bryn Mawr College, Bryn Mawr, Pa.
- 1 Mr. Carl Edelheim, 202 West Logan Square, Philadelphia, Pa.
- 1 Max Einhorn, M.D., 20 E. 63d St., New York.
- 1 Mr. F. Eissner, 18 Bible House, New York.
- 1 John F. Erdmann, M.D., 149 W. 44th St., New York.
- 1 His Excellency Athanasios P. Eutaxias, Minister of Cultus and Public Instruction of Greece, Athens, Greece.
- 1 Mr. B. Eutichidi, 914 Gravies St., New Orleans, La.
- 1 Miss Mary Evarts, 231 Second Ave., New York.
- 1 Rev. Wm. Everett, 44 Second Ave., New York.
- 1 W. A. Ewing, M.D., 134 W. 58th St., New York.
- 10 Mr. P. F. Fachiri, 145 W. 58th St., New York.
- 1 W. E. Farrar, Professor of Latin and Greek, Bethel College, Russellville, Ky.
- 1 Miss Louise M. Fitzgerald, 314 E. 30th St., New York.
- 1 Mr. Sophocles Fouriesos, 2260 St. Catherine St., Montreal, Canada.
- 1 Rev. James Fraser, Professor of Greek, New Windsor College, New Windsor, Maryland.
- 2 Francis Foerster, M.D., Professor Post-Graduate School of Medicine, New York.
- 1 G. R. Fowler, M.D., 301 De Kalb Ave., Brooklyn, N. Y.
- 1 W. Freudenthal, M.D., 1003 Madison Ave., New York.
- 1 J. Henry Fruitnight, M.D., 161 W. 57th St., New York.
- 1 Mr. C. S. Galanopoulo, 27½ Madison St., New York.
- 2 Mr. A. S. Galatti, Stegul Hotel, Temple, Texas.
- 2 Mr. P. J. Galatti, 15 Old Slip, New York.

No. of copies.

1 Deaconess Gardner, Grace Memorial Home, 94 Fourth Ave., New York.
1 Mrs. Mary R. Geis, 136th St., New York.
1 A. G. Gerster, M.D., Professor New York Polyklinik, New York.
1 Mr. E. W. Gilles, 120 E. 53d St., New York.
1 J. W. Gleitsmann, M.D., Professor Polyklinik, New York.
1 Mr. G. Georgopoulos, 33 S. William St., New York.
1 Rev. A. E. Gobble, President Central Pennsylvania College, New Berlin, Union Co., Pa.
1 Miss Caroline A. Godfroy, 366 Jefferson Ave., Detroit, Mich.
1 Dr. H. Goetter, 338 Second Ave., New York.
1 C. M. Gould, M.D., West Superior, Wis.
5 Dr. G., New York.
1 Miss Elisabeth Hatten, Professor Union Christian College, Merom, Sullivan Co., Ind.
2 Rev. F. Heiermann, S.J., Professor Canisius College, Buffalo, N. Y.
1 Messrs. Hunt & Gregorius, 259 First Ave., New York.
1 Rev. W. R. Huntington, Rector Grace Church, New York.
1 G. N. Hatzidakis, Professor of Philology, University Athens, Greece.
1 C. Imperatori, M.D., 28 Oliver St., New York.
1 A. V. Williams Jackson, Professor Columbia University, New York.
5 A. Jacobi, M.D., Professor Columbia University, New York.
1 George W. Jacoby, M.D., 663 Madison Ave., New York.
2 Mr. D. Jannopoulo, St. Louis, Mo.
1 Mr. George W. Jarchow, 445 Second Ave., New York.
1 S. S. Jones, M.D., 712 Madison Ave., New York.
1 Mr. Panagiotis D. Kalogeropoulos, Conservator of the Library of the Parliament, Athens, Greece.
1 Rev. Dr. Kalapothakis, Athens, Greece.
1 Mr. Petros Kannelidis, Editor of the Athenian *Daily Kairoi*, Athens.
1 Mr. John Kasimatis, 39 Odos Themistokleous, Athens, Greece.

LIST OF SUBSCRIBERS.

No. of copies.

- 1 P. Kastriotis, Ph.D., Ephoros Archaiotiton, Athens, Greece.
- 1 Mr. Starros Kazis, W. Blackstone St., opposite Old Boston and Maine Depot, Boston.
- 1 Alexander Kerr, Professor University of Wisconsin, Madison, Wis.
- 1 Kettembeil, M.D., 662 E. 146th St., New York.
- 2 Ed. L. Keyes, M.D., 109 E. 34th St., New York.
- 1 John B. Kieffer, Professor Franklin and Marshall College, Lancaster, Pa.
- 1 Mrs. Marie Kleman, 444 Central Park West, New York.
- 1 Rev. D. Kosionis, Greek Orthodox Church, Chicago, Ill.
- 1 Dr. Constantin Kourouniotis, Ephoros of the Archæological Society of Athens, Chios.
- 2 Mr. L. C. Kuchukoff, 41 E. 69th St., New York.
- 1 George F. Laidlaw, M.D., 137 W. 41st St., New York.
- 1 Mlle. Marie Lambert, 46 Seventh St., New York.
- 1 F. Lange, M.D., 130 E. 61st St., New York.
- 1 G. Langmann, M.D., 121 W. 57th St., New York.
- 1 Mr. Nicholas Laskaropoulos, 960 Lexington Ave., New York.
- 1 Charles A. Leale, M.D., 604 Madison Ave., New York.
- 2 Mr. John Lefferts, Jr., Lawyer, 186 Remsen St., Brooklyn, N. Y.
- 1 Mr. G. Lekas, 17 Roosevelt St., New York.
- 1 Dr. Basilios Leonardos, Ephoros of the Museum of Inscriptions, Athens, Greece.
- 1 Mr. Michael Likopantis, Athens, Greece.
- 1 Miss F. Margaret Linton, 414 E. 14th St., New York.
- 2 Mr. Gregory G. Livierato, 91–93 Wall St., New York.
- 1 Rudolf Loreck, Dr. Juris., Lawyer, 253 Broadway, New York.
- 1 Mr. Angelo Lucato, 301 Columbus Ave., New York.
- 1 Mr. J. E. McAfee, Parkville, Mo.
- 1 N. G. McMaster, M.D., 322 E. 15th St., New York.
- 2 Mr. John McClure, 259 W. 52d St., New York.
- 1 Rt. Rev. James A. McFaul, Bishop of Trenton, N. J.
- 1 John McNaugher, Professor Theological Seminary, Alleghany, Pa.

No. of copies.

- 1 Rev. Brother Maurice, President Rock Hill College, Ellicott City, Md.
- 1 Mr. John C. Maximus, Manhattan Club, cor. 34th St. and Fifth Ave., New York.
- 1 Mr. C. F. Mehltretter, 239 E. 87th St., New York.
- 2 Mr. C. Menelas, Mobile, Ala.
- 1 Mr. George Merck, 8th St., University Place, New York.
- 1 E. J. Messemer, M.D., 144 Second Ave., New York.
- 1 Mr. Max Meyer, Lawyer, 120 Broadway, New York.
- 1 Dr. Franz Meyer, Bound Brook, N. J.
- 1 Willy Meyer, M.D., Professor Post-Graduate School of Medicine, New York.
- 1 Mr. F. G. Miliadis, Augusta, Ga.
- 1 Mr. Miltiades A. Mitaranga, Waco, Texas.
- 1 Mrs. Bertha Morat, 321 E. 84th St., New York.
- 2 Rev. F. E. Murphy, S.J., President College of St. Francis Xavier, New York.
- 1 Right Rev. William F. Nichols, Bishop of California.
- 1 C. Nicolai, M.D., 81 W. 119th St., New York.
- 1 Mr. Nicholas Nikias, 960 Lexington Ave., New York.
- 1 Edward North, Professor Hamilton College, Clinton, N. Y.
- 1 Northwestern University Library, Watertown, Wis.
- 1 Harry S. Oppenheimer, M.D., 49 E. 23d St., New York.
- 1 Mrs. William Orlick, 51 E. 29th St., New York.
- 1 S. Stanhope Orris, Professor of Greek, Princeton University, Princeton, N. J.
- 1 F. A. Packard, M.D., Kearney, Neb.
- 3 Mr. John C. Palamaris, 117 S. Robey St., Chicago, Ill.
- 1 Th. Papadimitrakopoulos, Ph.D., Professor of Philology, University Athens, Greece.
- 1 Mr. Gregory D. Papadopulos, 828 Palace St., Montreal, Canada.
- 3 Rev. Archimandrit Agathodoros Papageorgopoulos, Rector Greek Church, New York.
- 1 Isaac A. Parker, Professor of Greek and Latin, Lombard University, Galesburg, Ill.
- 1 Mr. George Paspatis, 25 Odos Lykabiton, Athens, Greece.
- 1 Mrs. James Patterson, 23 Roosevelt St., New York.

LIST OF SUBSCRIBERS. 297

No. of copies.

- 1 Dred Peacock, President Greenboro Female College, Greenboro, N. C.
- 1 Charles R. Pepper, Professor Central University, Richmond, Ky.
- 1 Mlle. Marie Thérèse G. de la Perrière, Principal, Bridgeport, Conn.
- 1 Mr. Nicolas A. Petzalis, 35 Bd. du Port Royal, Paris, France.
- 1 Dr. Peterson, Superintendent McGill University College, Montreal, Canada.
- 1 Miss Caliopi Petimeza, Athens, Greece.
- 1 Mr. Constantine D. Phassoularidis, 960 Lexington Ave., New York.
- 1 Mr. William Phlippeau, Lawyer, 120 Broadway, New York.
- 1 Miss Adelais Phokaeos, Smyrna, Turkey.
- 10 Messrs. P. & R., New York.
- 1 Chester A. Place, President Southwest Kansas College, Winfield, Kans.
- 1 Mr. Louis Prang, Art Publisher, Roxbury, Boston, Mass.
- 1 Prof. Thomas R. Price, 263 W. 45th St., New York.
- 1 Mr. Berg. F. Prince, Springfield, O.
- 5 Messrs. Protopsalti Bros., Morley Ave., Nogales, Ariz.
- 1 Mr. Alcibiades Psiaki, 91–93 Wall St., New York.
- 1 Mrs. H. Purdy, 149 Lexington Ave., New York.
- 1 Mary Putnam-Jacobi, M.D., Professor Woman's College, New York.
- 1 Rev. James Quinn, Mt. Carmel, Tuxedo Park, N. Y.
- 3 Edward Quintard, M.D., 145 W. 58th St., New York.
- 1 Mr. John Rachiotis, 130 Tremont St., Boston, Mass.
- 1 Mrs. M. Rafter, 150 E. 27th St., New York.
- 1 Mr. Alexander A. Ralli, Waco, Texas.
- 5 Mr. Anthony P. Ralli, 15 Old Slip, New York.
- 5 Mr. Theodore P. Ralli, 15 Old Slip, New York.
- 1 C. A. v. Ramdohr, M.D., 45 Irving Place, New York.
- 1 Mr. G. Ramsperger, 236 E. 23d St., New York.
- 1 Mr. M. Rechnitzer, 387 St. Nicholas Ave., New York.
- 1 Thomas Richey, Professor of Ecclesiastical History, General Theological Seminary, New York.
- 2 Mr. Cæsar A. Roberts, 516 Cooper Building, Denver, Col.

No. of copies.

- 3 Mr. Herman Roder, 355 Central Ave., Jersey City Heights, N. J.
- 1 Mr. J. M. Rodocannachi, Boston, Mass.
- 1 His Highness Prince Demetrios Rodocanakis, Syra, Greece.
- 1 D. B. St. John Roosa, M.D., President Post-Graduate School of Medicine, New York.
- 3 Mr. William Sander, 1387 Lexington Ave., New York.
- 1 Mr. Thomas Schiadaressi, Augusta, Ga.
- 1 Mr. Julius C. Schlachter, 309 Jefferson Ave., Brooklyn, N. Y.
- 3 Mr. F. Schlesinger, 47 Third Ave., New York.
- 1 Mr. Theodore Schmalholz, Morristown, N. J.
- 1 Mrs. Ada Schmalholz, Morristown, N. J.
- 1 Mr. William Schmid, 1 W. 104th St., New York.
- 1 Mr. D. F. L. Schoenle, Bigelow Place, Mt. Auburn, Cincinnati, Ohio.
- 1 George Schroeder, M.D., Hohenhonnef-a.-Rh., Germany.
- 1 William J. Seelye, Professor of Greek University of Wooster, Wooster, Ohio.
- 1 N. Senn, M.D., Professor of Surgery, Chicago, Ill.
- 1 Blasius G. Skordeli, Ph.D., School Director, Athens, Greece.
- 1 Mr. H. E. Slagenhaup, Taneytown, Md.
- 1 Mr. Henry M. F. Smith, Rockland, Me.
- 1 A. H. Smith, M.D., Professor Post-Graduate School of Medicine, New York.
- 1 Mr. A. del Solar, 455 W. 22d St., New York.
- 1 Rev. Edward P. Southwell, O.C.C. Prior, Carmel Priory, 334 E. 29th St., New York.
- 1 Mr. G. Spiridis, 1 Odos Xanthou, Athens, Greece.
- 1 B. T. Spencer, Professor Kentucky Wesleyan College, Winchester, Ky.
- 4 Mr. Charles E. Sprague, President Union Dime Savings Bank, New York.
- 1 Mr. Alexander Starrides, 130 Tremont St., Boston, Mass.
- 1 Mr. Henry T. W. Steinberg, 434 E. 11th St., New York.
- 3 Clon Stephanos, M.D., Athens, Greece.
- 1 Franklin B. Stephenson, M.D., Surgeon United States Navy, Roxbury, Boston, Mass.
- 1 Miss J. D. Stewart, Iowa City, Iowa.

LIST OF SUBSCRIBERS.

No. of copies.

- 1 Rev. E. R. Stone, O.C.C., Carmel Priory, New York.
- 1 Joseph Edward Stubbs, President State University of Nevada, Reno, Nevada.
- 1 William F. Swahlen, Ph.D., Professor of Greek, De Pauw University, Greencastle, Ind.
- 1 Mrs. E. B. Thornton, 219 Second Ave., New York.
- 5 Hon. Demosthenes T. Timagenis, Consul of Greece in Boston, Mass.
- 2 Dr. Rudolf Tombo, 2 Ridge Pl., New York.
- 1 M. Toeplitz, M.D., 123 E. 62d St., New York.
- 1 Mr. Nic. S. Trakas, 620 Broad St., Augusta, Ga.
- 1 Mr. Stephen Vaitses, Melrose Highlands, Mass.
- 2 Messrs. George F. Vetter's Sons, 35 W. 23d St., New York.
- 1 Mr. A. L. K. Volkmann, 131 Davis Ave., Brookline, Mass.
- 2 Mr. Edw. H. Warker, Sheriff's Office, New York.
- 1 Mrs. Meta Weber, 25 West 46th St., New York.
- 2 Mr. Joseph F. Webber, 65 Fifth Ave., New York.
- 1 J. Shelly Weinberger, LL.D., Dean, and Professor of the Greek Language and Literature in Ursinus College, Collegeville, Pa.
- 1 Mrs. Ida V. Whitcomb, 1425 Holmes St., Kansas City, Mo.
- 1 Rev. N. White, D.D., Professor Lombard University, Galesburg, Ill.
- 1 Crosby C. Whitman, M.D., 166 W. 55th St., New York.
- 1 B. L. Wiggins, Vice-Chancellor University of the South, Sewanee, Tenn.
- 1 Lightner Whitmer, Ph.D., Professor University of Pennsylvania, Philadelphia, Ma.
- 1 Reynold Webb Wilcox, M.D., LL.D., Professor Post-Graduate School of Medicine, New York.
- 1 Mr. W. O. Wiley, 53 E. 10th St., New York.
- 1 W. P. Wilkin, M.D., 311 W. 46th St., New York.
- 1 Rev. Placidus Wingerter, O.S.B., Professor St. John's University, Collegeville, Minn.
- 1 George Edward Woodberry, Professor Columbia University, New York.
- 1 Dr. B. D. Woodward, of the Department of Romance Languages, Columbia University, New York.

No. of copies.
- 1 L. C. Woolery, Professor West Virginia University, Morgantown, W. Va.
- 2 Messrs. Wray & Pilsbury, Lawyers, 237 Broadway, New York.
- 1 Mr. Leonidas Zacharakos, 34 Madison St., New York.
- 1 Th. Zaimis, M.D., Patras, Greece.
- 1 Mr. Francis J. Zitz, 1272 Broadway, New York.
- 1 Mr. William Zobel, 217 Mercer St., New York.
- 1 Mr. Alexandros F. Zographas, 148 E. 30th St., New York.
- 1 Denison University Library (R. S. Colwell, Chairman), Granville, Ohio.
- 1 Messrs. Notara Bros., 1215 Broadway, New York.
- 1 Sherman Kirk, Professor of Greek, 1084, 25th St., Des Moines, Iowa.
- 1 Mr. Demosthenes D. Desminis, Athens, Greece.
- 1 Sidney G. Ashmore, Professor of Latin, Union College, Schenectady, N. Y.

www.ingramcontent.com/pod-product-compliance
Lightning Source LLC
Chambersburg PA
CBHW031901220426
43663CB00006B/718